JAN
HERMANN

D0925321

AEROFILMS GUIDE

The
Cotswold Way

Ted Fryer

IAN ALLAN
Publishing

THE COTSWOLD WAY

Based on an original idea by
Richard Cox of Aerofilms

Designer Michael D. Stride
Series Editor Rebecca King

Published by Ian Allan Ltd, Shepperton, Surrey;
and printed by Ian Allan Printing Ltd at their
works at Coombelands in Runnymede, England

Text © Ian Allan Ltd 1992
Photographs © Aerofilms 1992
(unless otherwise credited)

The publishers gratefully acknowledge the
following for the use of photographs.
AA Photo Library: pages 4, 5, 31, 42, 43, 52,
53, 58, 59, 66, 67, 74, 75, 87, 96, 97, 106,
107, 117; Nature Photographers Ltd: pages
36, 37, 96, 97.

Features by Richard Cavendish

While every effort has been taken to ensure
the accuracy of the information in this
book, the publishers cannot accept
responsibility for errors or omissions, or for
changes in details given.

First published 1992

ISBN 0 7110 2041 8

All rights reserved. No part of this book may be
reproduced or transmitted in any form or by any
means, electronic or mechanical, including photo-
copying, recording or by any information storage
and retrieval system, without permission from the
Publisher in writing.

Contents

Inset: Near Lower Hamswell
Main picture: The Air Balloon pub near
Barrow Wake
Title page: Tyndale Monument,
North Nibley

Other titles in this series:
The South Downs Way
The South Devon Coast Path

Followir

The Cotswold Way is generally very well waymarked
As well as the standard system of painted arrows –
yellow for a footpath, blue for a bridleway – a white
spot is used to indicate the route of the Way. Where

SECTIONS OF THE WAY

The route from Chipping
Campden to Bath has been
divided into sections that can
comfortably be walked in a
day. Each of these sections
opens with an introduction
and the distance involved is
given.

VERTICAL PHOTO-MAPS

Every step of the Way is
plotted on vertical
photographs using a scale of
1:10,000 (1 miles:6.5ins,
1km:10cm).

COMPASS POINT

Every photo-map is
accompanied by a compass
point for ease of orientation.

OBLIQUE PHOTOGRAPHS

These photographs bring a
new perspective to the
landscape and its buildings.
All the subjects chosen can
either be seen from, lie on, or
are within easy reach of the
Way.

SCALE FOR PHOTO-MAPS

The scale-bar represents a
distance of 0.310 miles
(0.5km).

Chipping Campden to Stanton
10 miles (16km)

From Chipping Campden the Way leads over the High Wold
through classic north Cotswold villages of warm stone, built with
the wealth from the wool trade and later restored by
dedicated newcomers. There are fine
views in all directions.

*Chipping Campden, one of the finest of the
wool towns, has a charter dating back to 1180*

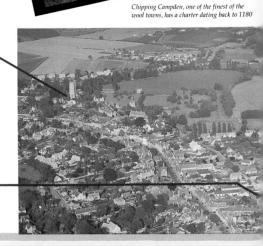

The vertical photography used in the photo-maps is taken from an
average height above sea level. This means that the scale of the
photography will alter slightly as the contours of the ground vary.
The photo-maps are constructed by piecing together a series of
photographs to make each page. They are intended to give a

e Route

e Way follows roads or green lanes, a white arrow is
sed. Waymarks may be found on indicator plinths or
ooden signposts, or they may be stamped on a post
stile.

COTSWOLD WAY starts officially
e marker stone beside the town hall
hipping Campden, but the walker
like to begin this 100-mile (160km)
rimage to the great abbey church in
at the humbler parish church of St
es which, for its size, is an equally
source of interest. A fine brass in
t of the altar commemorates

William Grevel — 'the Flower of the
Wool Merchants of All England'.

The curving High Street includes
Grevel's House (1380) and the gabled
and arcaded Market Hall (1627), which
was rescued from export to America in
the 1940s. The Woolstapler's Hall, now a
museum, was where the wool
merchants traded — creating the wealth
with which the town was built.

Dover's Hill, rescued from hotel
development in the 1920s, belongs to the
National Trust. It has become famous
for the 'Cotswold Olympicks', instituted
by Robert Dover in 1612 and now an
annual event held on the Friday after
Spring Bank Holiday. Proceedings
culminate in a torchlight procession into
the town.

On a fine day the view ranges from
the Malvern Hills to Shropshire's Clee
Hills, and over the Warwickshire plain
towards Birmingham.

GENERAL TEXT
Places to visit, points of
specific interest and
information relevant to that
particular stretch of the route
accompanies every photo-
map. The Heart of England
Tourist Board (see page 120)
will supply opening times to
places to visit, and it is
always advisable to check
details in advance of a visit to
avoid disappointment.
Generally, opening times
between October and Easter
are very limited.

SYMBOLS
The following symbols
appear on the photo-maps for
information and to help the
walker get his bearings.

![railway]	Railway station
![viewpoint]	Viewpoint
★	Place of interest
![pub]	Pub or hotel
P	Car park
![church]	Church

ROUTE DIRECTIONS
These numbered route
directions correspond to the
numbers shown in yellow on
the photo-maps. Sometimes
alternative paths or optional
diversions are given.

OUTE DIRECTIONS

rom the church walk beside the almhouses.
right, pass the Eight Bells Inn, then turn left
the High Street. At the town hall cross the
into the square at the Cotswold Way marker
e.

urn right past St Catherine's RC Church into
t End Terrace. Where the road turns right,

bear up the hill into Hoo Lane. If the bridleway is
muddy use the footpath on the left.

3. Turn left along the road for a few yards before
turning right into a field. Cross the stile on to
Dover's Hill. Walk forward to the scarp edge and
follow its rim, left, to the topograph.

4. From the topograph walk through the car park
and down the entry drive on to the road. Turn left
and, at the crossroads, turn right to walk beside
the road to a stone stile.

11

pictorial representation of the ground and strict accuracy of scale
throughout cannot be guaranteed. There may also be a mismatch
in areas of extreme relief – ie where the land is steepest. These
problems have been kept to a minimum, in particular close to the
main route of the walk.

Practical Information

ACCOMMODATION AND TRANSPORT

The Cotswold Way frequently passes through villages and small towns, and where it does cross an emptier landscape it is rarely more than a mile or two from a road. Since the bus services linking the villages are reasonable, if not always what might be termed frequent, the walker who does not wish to tackle the route with a rucksack can always find food and accommodation.

British Rail stations near the Way include Evesham, Moreton-in-Marsh, Cheltenham, Gloucester, Stroud, Stonehouse and Bath.

All the towns, and many of the villages, have hotels and those that do not usually offer a bed and breakfast service. Whether you will need to book depends on when you intend to walk. In high season there may well be 'No Vacancies' signs in most windows as the Cotswolds are a popular tourist area, but out of season there should be little problem.

The Gloucestershire branch of the Ramblers' Association produces a very useful booklet, *The Cotswold Way Handbook*, which contains information about accommodation of all kinds, as well as travel information. It can be obtained from the Cotswold Countryside Service or the Ramblers' Association (see page 120).

COUNTRY CODE

Enjoy the countryside and respect its life and work
Guard against all risk of fire
Fasten all gates
Keep dogs under close control
Keep to public paths across farmland
Use gates and stiles to cross fences, hedges and walls
Leave livestock crops and machinery alone
Take your litter home
Help to keep all water clean
Protect wildlife, plants and trees
Take special care on country roads; keep to the right and walk in single file
Make no unnecessary noise

BEFORE YOU GO

Careful planning and appropriate clothing are the keys to enjoyable walking. Although the Cotswold Way poses no real problems in terms of

Dursley

terrain or weather conditions, walkers should wear tough, non-slip footwear as there are some steep slopes which can become very greasy, and there are also some muddy sections. Always take a lightweight waterproof and carry enough food and drink for the day. Allow yourself plenty of time and, as optional extras, pack a pair of binoculars, a good field guide or two and a compass.

RIGHTS OF WAY

There are two main kinds of public rights of way: footpaths, open to walkers only, and bridleways, open to

by established custom or consent, and these include country parks and picnic sites, beaches, canal towpaths, some woodlands and forests, particularly those owned by the Forestry Commission, and many areas of open country. For more information about walking and the law contact the Countryside Commission (address on page 120). It is worth remembering that hedges and fences can be removed, rights of way re-routed, paths become very overgrown, and in wet weather conditions streams and rivers may be impassable.

AEROFILMS LIMITED

Aerofilms was founded in 1919 and has specialised in the acquisition of aerial photography within the United Kingdom throughout its history. The company has a record of being innovative in the uses and applications of aerial photography.

Photographs looking at the environment in perspective are called oblique aerial photographs. These photographs are taken with Hasselblad cameras by professional photographers experienced in the difficult conditions encountered in aerial work.

Photographs looking straight down at the landscape are termed vertical aerial photographs. These photographs are obtained by using Leica survey cameras, the products from which are normally used in the making of maps.

Aerofilms has a unique library of oblique and vertical photographs in excess of one and a half million covering the United Kingdom. This library of photographs dates from 1919 to the present and is continually being updated.

Oblique and vertical photography can be taken to customers' specification by Aerofilms' professional photographers. Due to the specific nature of the requirements of the Aerofilms guides, new photography has been taken for these books.

To discover more of the wealth of past or present photographs held in the library at Aerofilms, including photographs in this guide, or to commission new aerial photography to your requirements, please contact:

Aerofilms Limited
Gate Studios
Station Road
Borehamwood
Herts
WD6 1EJ
Telephone: 081-207 0666
Fax: 081-207 5433

walkers, horse-riders and bicycle-riders. Footpaths are sometimes waymarked with a yellow dot and bridleways with a blue dot. Another category is byways, or 'roads used as a public path', and these can be used by walkers, horse-riders, cyclists, and may have vehicular access.

It is permissible to take a pram, pushchair or wheelchair along rights of way, and a dog if kept under control. You are also entitled to make a short detour around an obstruction, or remove it in order to get past.

There are also a number of other areas to which the public are allowed access

Painswick hillfort

Introduction to the Cotswold Way

Unusually for a long-distance footpath, the Cotswold Way seeks out villages and towns. At first this seems to be a contradiction: surely walkers on such routes are looking to get back to nature, to be away from the works of man? Normally that is true, as most long-distance paths cross wild upland areas where evidence of man is scarce. In the Cotswolds the situation is different as the entire landscape has been created by man, but this in itself gives the walk a special charm and interest.

The earliest evidence of occupation is the Neolithic long barrows, two fine examples of which lie on the Way. These burial mounds were created by forming huge slabs of rock into box-like chambers and earthing them over. Some 1,500 years later, when the Saxons farmed the High Wolds, as the upland plains are known, a chieftain living near the source of

the Windrush, close to Winchcombe, named the area. He was Cod, pronounced 'code', and the local land became known as Cod's Wold.

In medieval times wool was the basis of England's wealth and sheep fared well on the Cotswolds, producing a heavy fleece that made a sought-after wool. At first the wool was exported, but it was soon evident that sending wool abroad and importing expensive cloth made poor economics, and groups of Flemish weavers were persuaded to ply their trade in the Cotswolds. To the east of the Way near Hawkesbury Upton are the villages of Dunkirk and Petty France, sure signs of a Flemish presence.

The wool merchants grew fabulously rich and competed with each other to display their wealth. This resulted in the magnificent 'wool' churches of the area – the

Way passes close to several – which are set in villages built of local stone that are equally pleasing. We owe the wholeness of these villages to the dramatic decline of the wool trade in the 17th century. The area's prosperity dwindled and, as it was poorly positioned to benefit from the Industrial Revolution, there was little new building. A sad irony of the decline of the trade was that soldiers were needed to quell the riots of starving weavers in some areas. One of these was Stroud, where the red cloth for the soldiers' uniforms, the red of the 'thin red line', had been made.

Occasionally the Cotswolds are referred to as hills, and if the area is viewed from east of the River Severn it does indeed look like a long, low range of hills. But hills the Cotswolds are not: in fact they consist of a limestone escarpment with a long dip slope, the steep scarp face being the visible feature. The Cotswold Way takes the edge of that scarp, keeping to high ground as it explores the area from Chipping Campden at the northern extremity to Bath where the scarp face finally ends. It is a gentle route, falling into the occasional scarp-splitting valley, but only rarely requiring a steep climb out again. High Cleeve Hill, the highest point of the Cotswolds, can be windswept, but in general the Way is not exposed and provides easy walking with ample opportunities to stop and enjoy a taste of medieval England.

Cam Long Down

Inset: Stanway House

Chipping Campden to Stanton

10 miles (16km)

From Chipping Campden the Way leads over the High Wold
through classic north Cotswold villages of warm stone, built with
the wealth from the wool trade and later restored by
dedicated newcomers. There are fine
views in all directions.

CHIPPING CAMPDEN

*Chipping Campden, one of the finest of the
wool towns, has a charter dating back to 1180*

THE COTSWOLD WAY starts officially at the marker stone beside the town hall in Chipping Campden, but the walker may like to begin this 100-mile (160km) pilgrimage to the great abbey church in Bath at the humbler parish church of St James which, for its size, is an equally rich source of interest. A fine brass in front of the altar commemorates William Grevel — 'the Flower of the Wool Merchants of All England'.

The curving High Street includes Grevel's House (1380) and the gabled and arcaded Market Hall (1627), which was rescued from export to America in the 1940s. The Woolstapler's Hall, now a museum, was where the wool merchants traded — creating the wealth with which the town was built.

Dover's Hill, rescued from hotel development in the 1920s, belongs to the National Trust. It has become famous for the 'Cotswold Olympicks', instituted by Robert Dover in 1612 and now an annual event held on the Friday after Spring Bank Holiday. Proceedings culminate in a torchlight procession into the town.

On a fine day the view ranges from the Malvern Hills to Shropshire's Clee Hills, and over the Warwickshire plain towards Birmingham.

ROUTE DIRECTIONS

1. From the church walk beside the almhouses. Turn right, pass the Eight Bells Inn, then turn left into the High Street. At the town hall cross the road into the square at the Cotswold Way marker stone.

2. Turn right past St Catherine's RC Church into West End Terrace. Where the road turns right, bear up the hill into Hoo Lane. If the bridleway is muddy use the footpath on the left.

3. Turn left along the road for a few yards before turning right into a field. Cross the stile on to Dover's Hill. Walk forward to the scarp edge and follow its rim, left, to the topograph.

4. From the topograph walk through the car park and down the entry drive on to the road. Turn left and, at the crossroads, turn right to walk beside the road to a stone stile.

1. At the stone stile turn left, then turn right beside the copse and enter the long strip of land of 11 acres (4.5 hectares) called the Mile Drive. This is sometimes cultivated.

2. Walk the length of this to another stone stile. Beyond this, the path crosses two fields to reach the road (Buckle Street). Cross the field opposite, to enter the Fish Hill picnic area, where there are toilets.

THE MILE DRIVE

IN THE GREAT DAYS of the English wool industry, some 600 years ago, the land to the left of the Way would have been used as sheep pasture. At that time the sheep grazing here were 'Cotswold Lions', descendants of a breed introduced by the Romans. The length, or staple, of its wool was longer than many other breeds and much prized. There was a saying that 'in Europe the best wool is English, and in England the best wool is Cotswold'. Now much of the land is cultivated for crops although economic requirements change, and in recent years more sheep have been seen again on these hills as the European Community demands less corn production.

Buckle Street is an old Saxon road from Bourton-on-the-Water. Just north of Campden it joins the Roman Ryknield Street, which runs from Bourton to Birmingham and Wall (*Letocetum*) on Watling Street, now the A5, and beyond.

The paths either side of Buckle Street are the first of many which cross fields rather than follow field edges, showing that rights of way often predate current boundaries. Waymarking indicates that you have the right to cross such fields, even if crops are growing, provided you keep to the route indicated.

Fish Hill picnic area was opened in 1974 on the site of an old Cotswold stone quarry. The site is owned by the County Council, as is the woodland below where there are nature trails. The topograph is finely carved, but there is little view to admire.

Chipping Campden is left behind as the Way heads over Dover's Hill and along the Mile Drive

James Wyatt designed Broadway Tower in the late 18th century. It commands a view of 12 counties on a clear day

TRAFFIC USING Fish Hill travels fast these days — unlike the time when extra horses had to be used to draw carriages up it. The hill was a noted trial run for cars in the early days of motoring.

Broadway Tower, a folly built by the Earl of Coventry at the end of the 18th century, was said to be visible from the family's property at Croome, west of Pershore. In the 19th century the tower — part of the Middle Hill estate — belonged to a notable book-collector, Thomas Phillips, who housed a printing press in it. He acquired so many volumes that parts of the collection are still being auctioned off 100 years on! Later the tower was let as a holiday cottage and among its visitors were artists such as William Morris, Burne-Jones and Rosetti. One of Morris's letters written from here resulted in the foundation of the Society for the Preservation of Ancient Buildings. Today, as part of the country park, the tower houses exhibitions and has a viewing gallery. The tower stands on the top of Broadway, or Beacon Hill which, at 1,024ft (312m), is one of the highest points of the Cotswolds. There are splendid views.

The main village street of Broadway, with its antique shops, pubs and tea rooms, attracts visitors in their hundreds. The Lygon Arms Hotel is one of the original coaching inns. Formerly known as the White Horse Inn, it was renamed when General Lygon arrived in the area after the Battle of Waterloo. Just down the street, off the village green, the Broadway Hotel is based on a 14th-century house. Off the main street, behind a high hedge near the turn into the Snowshill road, lies the 14th-century Abbot's Grange (now a private house), a retreat of the Abbots of Pershore who owned much of Broadway.

Follow the waymarks across two open fields to the wicket-gate by Broadway Tower.

1. From the topograph walk to the main road. Take care crossing. Follow the waymarks, turn left into the wood and follow the track to a field gate.

2. Turn sharp right and follow the footpath downhill to leave the country park through a gate. Note: except on the public footpaths, there is no public access to the country park without paying the admission charge at the tower or the main gate. The park is only open at weekends in the winter.

3. Follow the wall, passing Clump Farm on the right. The farm is so called because of a clump of decaying beech trees. The National Trust has planted a replacement clump close by. Continue through several fields to reach an alleyway leading to the main street in Broadway.

4. Turn left, and walk down the 'broad way' to the war memorial. By the village green turn left into the Snowshill road. Just beyond the church turn right and continue to a footbridge.

BROADWAY

N

GEOLOGY AND LANDSCAPE

THE COTSWOLDS lie on the landscape like a wedge of cheese on its side. The thick edge is the steep escarpment to the west, running for 50 miles (80.5km) or so and rising to above 1,000ft (304.5m) at its highest points. It commands serene and spacious views to the Malvern Hills, the River Severn and the mountains of Wales. Down below this limestone escarpment is the clay of the Vale of Severn with its lush green fields and orchards, running south-west from Evesham and Tewkesbury past Cheltenham and Gloucester. Going eastwards from the Cotswolds 'edge' is the 'dip', the long gradual slope which tilts gently down until the Cotswolds peter out towards Oxford and the Thames.

The Cotswolds are part of the great limestone belt that runs diagonally across England from the North Sea to the Dorset coast. All landscape has its distant origins in geology and the Cotswolds scenery goes back to the Jurassic period, roughly 140 to 200 million years ago, when the area lay beneath the sea. Over an immensity of time beds of clay, sand and limestone formed and when the sea receded, the limestone was left on the surface of the hills.

The upper limestone layers are of oolite, the enchanting Cotswolds building stone. Below are liassic rocks, which in valleys lie beneath rich green pastureland. A terrace of liassic rock called marlstone runs along at the foot of the Cotswold edge, containing springs which account for a line of

Drakestone Point
Charlton Kings Common

towns and villages from Chipping
Campden to Wotton-under-Edge and
beyond.

The steep western scarp, with its
beautiful beechwoods, is being steadily
eroded by wind and weather, and is
very slowly receding. Some hills have
become detached from the scarp as
outliers, Bredon Hill is one, and in the
south Stinchcombe Hill is almost
completely separated.

Streams have cut steep, narrow
valleys through the escarpment, notably
the River Frome, which has carved the
spectacular Golden valley, where the
canal and the railway line run from
Sapperton to Stroud. There are also
'hanging' valleys – secluded, narrow
and dry – so called because they hang
above the river valleys. They were
formed by melting ice in the Ice Age.

Up on the dip slope is one of
England's classic country landscapes, a
rolling upland plateau with deep
valleys, patches of woodland and broad,
sheep-nibbled pastures. Villages shelter
on the lower slopes and in the valleys.
Drystone walls stretch away for miles,
following the contours, and farmhouses
and cottages in the local stone seem as
natural an element on the scene as if
they had grown instead of being built.

BUCKLAND

THE BADSEY BROOK cuts into the Cotswolds here and flows on to the village from which it takes its name, near Evesham. From there it flows into the Avon, which in turn joins the Severn.

Broadway Coppice lies on the ridge and its name recalls the traditional method of managing woodland, coppice-with-standard, that was practised in nearly all British woodlands until earlier this century. Large trees, the standards, were allowed to grow to their full height for a considerable number of years and in between coppiced trees and shrubs, usually hazel, were cut back to the ground on a regular basis to produce thinner stems. Although much woodland has been neglected since the advent of cheap imports, several hazel coppices can still be seen and the wood has a wide number of uses. One of the results of coppicing and pollarding — cutting back growth above the height of grazing animals — is to prolong the life of trees almost indefinitely and their gnarled, misshapen trunks may be hundreds of years old. Another spin-off from woodland management is the wide variety of wildlife habitats it creates.

Several villages lie at the foot of the scarp below the Way between Broadway and Winchcombe and at one time they were owned by the monasteries. Buckland, the first of these passed by the Way, belonged to Gloucester. The village church has accumulated a number of treasures over the centuries, including 15th-century glass, seating dating from the days when these parishes were fiercely Protestant, a gallery, a maple-wood mazer (drinking bowl) and an Arts and Crafts reredos, which commemorates a First World War casualty.

ROUTE DIRECTIONS

1. Cross the bridge to the road. Cross this and follow the Way on the fenced path to the upper field. Walk up the side of the field, turning left at the top to reach a wicket-gate.

2. Enter Broadway Coppice, bearing right uphill. Turn left to a wicket-gate into a field and follow the hedge on the left. Continue over the stile in the same direction to reach a track.

3. Turn left along the track for some distance to reach a gate, then turn right to another gate. Continue past farm buildings on the left.

The isolated hill village of Snowshill lies east of the scarp

THE RIDGED GROUND seen to the right of the Way forms part of the remains of Shenberrow hillfort. This is the first of several forts on our route, but there are more impressive examples to come. On the hillside to the right of the track into Stanton can be seen the Guildhouse, built in traditional Cotswold style 30 years ago by Mary Osborn as part of a scheme to preserve rural crafts in the community. Today craft courses are run here.

Many of the stone buildings in Stanton (the name comes from 'stan tun', meaning stony farm) had fallen into disrepair by the early part of this century, but Sir Philip Stott, an architect,

spent the last 30 years of his life, and much of his wealth, restoring the village. Fortunately, subsequent housing has been built in traditional Cotswold style, using traditional materials, so the overall effect remains uniformly pleasing. The Mount Inn is a pleasant place in which to seek refreshment, and a glance inside the church reveals the work of Sir Ninian Comper.

Snowshill Manor dates from the Tudor period although its facade was added in the early 18th century. Fascinating collections ranging from Japanese armour to toys fill the rooms, and there is a small formal garden. It is owned by the National Trust.

STANTON

ROUTE DIRECTIONS

1. Continue through a gate and on to a crosstrack. This is the old road between Stanton (right) and Snowshill (left). Turn left, and then right through another gate.

2. Ignore the next track on the left and continue ahead to Shenberrow hillfort. Leave the track to reach an iron gate, walk ahead then turn right down a steep-sided valley.

3. On nearing the wall ahead bear left over a stile. Turn right to follow the field boundary, cross back over a stile, and descend to a pool. Bear right by the pool and turn left across two stiles by the water tanks. Follow the track down to Stanton village, taking the lane to the right to join the main street. (The Mount Inn provides welcome refreshment up the street to the right.)

4. The Way turns left down to the next junction. Turn left, follow the signs ahead on to a track bearing left and go through the fence on the right.

5. Cross the field and go over a stile to the right of a gate. After another stile, cross the fields over a double stile, go through a gate and bear right to a stile and into the parkland of Stanway House (see page 24).

PREHISTORIC COTSWOLDS

The first human beings to set foot in the Cotswolds area were nomadic hunters, paddling along the rivers in dugout canoes and moving from camp to camp through the forests as they stalked game. The first to settle down and live in one place were New Stone Age farmers, more than 5,000 years ago. Their pigs fed on the beech mast in the woods and they grew their crops in clearings.

These farming people began the human transformation of the Cotswolds landscape by clearing the forests with axe and fire. They left striking monuments behind them in the great tombs which lie like stranded whales in commanding positions on the hills. It was probably chieftains and their families who were interred in these long barrows, which were also shrines where the ancestors of the clan or the tribe were honoured. A huge mound of earth was piled up over the stone chambers in which the bodies of the dead were placed. There was usually an imposing doorway at one end with a forecourt protected by curved stretches of drystone walling, shaped like horns and constructed using the same basic techniques as drystone walls today.

Perhaps the most impressive of them all is Belas Knap, silent and eerie above Winchcombe. Above Wotton-under-Edge are Hetty Pegler's Tump (or Uley Tumulus) and Nympsfield long barrow which has lost its covering mound, so that the interior can be seen.

Later, in the Bronze Age, the dead were buried in smaller, less impressive round barrows, often in groups. There is a cluster of them at Snowshill and another at Temple Guiting. Much later still, in the Iron Age, powerful hillforts

Cleeve Common hillfort

Belas Knap long barrow, south-west of Winchcombe, dates back some 4,000 years

were constructed all along the Cotswolds scarp and their earthwork defences still loom up on the skyline today. They suggest a period of greatly increased warfare, raiding and cattle rustling. There is a particularly fine one at Little Sodbury, with double ramparts and ditches on three sides. The fort at Uleybury covers about 30 acres (12 hectares), perched above 300ft (94m) drops on three sides.

The smaller forts were probably chieftains' strongholds to which the local people could retreat when raiders or war parties were sighted. A fort like this originally had a wooden gateway, topped by a row of human heads grinning on poles, for the Celtic people who built them were head-hunters.

The bigger forts enclosed villages or small towns, like Crickley Hill, which held rectangular houses up to 60ft (18.2m) long, smaller houses and storage huts. A large roundhouse may have been the great hall of the local chief or king. These were the people the Romans conquered.

Little Down is the most southerly hillfort on the Way

Stanton to Cleeve Common

13 miles (21km)

**This interesting section
of the Way passes handsome Stanway House,
the ruins of Hailes Abbey and Winchcombe with its
Roman villa, before reaching the windswept 'uplands' of Cleeve
Common. The last few miles are quite strenuous.**

ON REACHING THE ROAD into the village of Stanway look across to the thatched cricket pavilion built by the playwright James Barrie when he lived at Stanton House. The staddle stones beneath it are a familiar sight in the Cotswolds as many barns were raised in this way to prevent rats reaching the grain.

Stanway House is open on certain days in the summer. It was built by the Tracy family in the 17th century and the gatehouse features the scallop shells of their family emblem. Inside is a jumble of passageways, tiny lobbies and charming rooms furnished with family heirlooms and portraits. Rents from estate tenants are still received in the traditional manner in the audit room. A huge 14th-century tithe barn, built for Tewkesbury Abbey, stands in the grounds.

Stanway House and the village church, which was largely rebuilt in Victorian times

ROUTE DIRECTIONS

1. Cross the avenue of trees on the Stanway Estate diagonally to reach the road.

2. Follow the road to the left, past Stanway church and house. At the gatehouse turn right, then turn left past some cottages. Go through a kissing-gate, and continue around the outside of the estate yard to a track. Turn left to the road.

3. Turn left for a few yards and cross to the path on the right. Follow the right-hand hedge to Wood Stanway. Turn left up the lane and bear left into the fields above. The diversion notice and waymarks indicate the route through fields to the right of the farm to join a track for a short distance before bearing right uphill. Turn left and right with the wall, then diverge left to reach the road at Stumps Cross. The stump of the cross is still visible by the wall.

4. Immediately turn right. Follow the track to a copse, turn right, then go left through a gate. Turn right, following the right-hand wall to the field corner, then turn left to a gate.

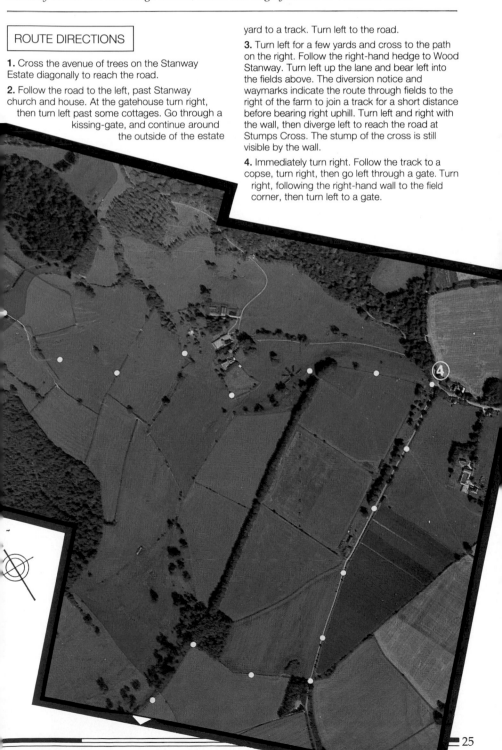

BECKBURY CAMP is another of the Iron Age forts built on the scarp. The embankments mark the remains of the defences and from them it is possible to obtain a clear idea of the size of the original settlement — about 4 acres (1.6 hectares). The trees and the monument on the fort are called Cromwell's Clump and Cromwell's Seat respectively, in memory of the story that Thomas Cromwell rested here to oversee the dismantling of Hailes Abbey below. (The abbey is now not visible because of the trees.) Hailes Abbey, a National Trust property, is managed by English Heritage and kept open all year. Apart from the lovely ruined cloisters, there is a covered display area on the site containing some carved stonework from the abbey of very high quality. A small museum has medieval tiles, clay pipes, pottery and various other artefacts recovered from the site. The church to the right of the abbey is also worth visiting for its medieval wall paintings, the best of which include a figure of St Christopher and a hunting scene.

ROUTE DIRECTIONS

1. Continue to Beckbury Camp. At the clump of trees go through the gate then walk left across the field to a gate. Cross the next two fields to a track. Turn right and go past the fruit farm to Hailes Abbey.

2. Just beyond the abbey go through a gate on the left. Cross the field to another gate and take the track to the road.

3. Turn right, pass a bungalow, then turn left on to a track. Go through two gates, walk past the first field on the right, then turn right along the hedge to a sign pointing across the field.

All that remains of Hailes Abbey, one of the last Cistercian abbeys to be built in England

N

WINCHCOMBE WAS ONE of the capitals of the Kingdom of Mercia, with a prosperous abbey that existed, with mixed fortune, for over 700 years. Its abbey stood on the site behind the wall on Abbey Terrace. Today the town is thriving with a choice of places for refreshment, though the George has recently been converted into apartments. When the front door is open, passers-by can still see the medieval staircase and gallery to the rooms of the old inn, frequented by pilgrims on their way to Hailes Abbey. A small folk museum is housed in the old town hall in the High Street and in Gloucester Street there is a railway museum. The museum garden features a Victorian vegetable garden and a medieval garden of medicinal herbs. On Abbey Terrace a signpost shows the junction of several long-distance routes.

The Wychavon Way covers 40 miles (64km) to reach the Severn near Droitwich, and the Wardens' Way (through villages), and the Windrush Way (over the High Wold), both go to Bourton-on-the-Water to join the Oxfordshire Way on its journey to the Thames. We take the Wardens' Way to the entrance to Sudeley Castle. Vineyard Street is also known as Duck Street because of the ducking-stool placed there in less enlightened days to punish over-talkative women! Sudeley Castle was home to Catherine Parr, sixth wife of Henry VIII, who married Thomas Seymour after Henry's death. She is buried here. During the Civil War the castle was slighted, and

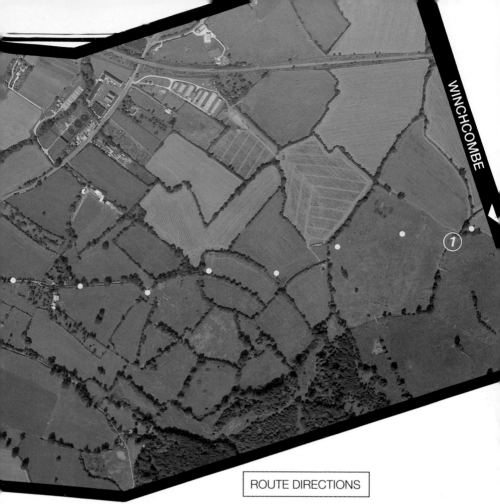

①

ROUTE DIRECTIONS

1. Continue across fields to a track which leads to the A46. Turn left to reach Winchcombe, where many waymarks are painted on the kerbstones.

2. Stay on the main road to reach Abbey Terrace where there is car parking. Beyond this turn left down Vineyard Street towards Sudeley Castle.

3. At the entrance to the castle turn along the road to the right. At the signpost on the right cross the fields diagonally.

left a ruin. Its fortunes revived in the 19th century when the Dent family, of glove-making fame, rebuilt and refurbished it. They also built almshouses and a school in the town. The castle is open from spring to autumn.

The A46 winds through the small town of Winchcombe, the former capital of a Saxon shire

THE ROMANS IN THE COTSWOLDS

The Romans invaded England in AD43 and swiftly took control of most of the south and east of the country, which they named Britannia. They seem to have had little trouble with the natives of the Cotswolds, a Celtic tribe which they called the *Dobunni*. The Foss Way marks the Roman initial frontier, running from Exeter to Bath and across the southern Cotswolds, into Cirencester on today's A433 and out again on the line of the A429 for Leicester and Lincoln. At Cirencester it crossed another Roman road, Ermine Street, coming from the south-east. Today's A417 follows it as straight as an arrow across the Cotswold slopes to Birdlip, and from there it ran on to Gloucester.

Gloucester was the Roman *Glevum*, a legionary fortress at a strategic point on the Severn, which grew into a sizeable town. Finds from Roman times are in the City Museum and parts of the city

The foundations of the villa at Witcombe, with the bath house contained in huts

wall and the east gate can be seen.

Up on the Cotswolds the Roman peace encouraged substantial estates to flourish, each centred on a luxurious house, or villa. The most impressive one is at Chedworth, not far from the Foss Way. Forgotten for centuries, it was rediscovered in 1864 by a gamekeeper digging for a strayed ferret. The mosaic floor on the theme of the seasons has survived the centuries and there are remains of two suites of baths, numerous rooms and the underfloor central heating system. There is less to see at Great Witcombe Roman Villa, near Cooper's Hill, with a bath suite and rooms ranged round an open courtyard.

One of the most luxurious villas of Roman Britain was discovered at Woodchester, south of Stroud, with 65 rooms and a huge mosaic of Orpheus playing his lyre to the animals and birds, 46ft (14m) square and made of 1.5 million pieces. This is occasionally shown to the public, but only at long intervals and nothing else is visible at the site. A replica of the mosaic is in the

Tabernacle church at Wotton-under-Edge.

Far and away the most important and impressive Roman remains in the area are those at Bàth, where recent archeological work has uncovered more of the spa of *Aquae Sulis*, with its lavish baths and temple complex. A mass of everyday objects, inscriptions and offerings made at the sacred spring, with mosaics and sculptures including the famous Gorgon's head pediment and a lifesize bronze head of the goddess Minerva, can be admired at a site which is a 'must' for visitors.

Chedworth's underfloor heating system and a detail of the villa's Four Seasons mosaic. Finds and plans of the site are displayed in a museum nearby

Belas Knap long barrow

ROUTE DIRECTIONS

1. After crossing two field boundaries and a footbridge, bear right round the field edge to a stile then turn left.

2. Continue to the left of Wadfield House and the farm buildings. Follow the track, to the right of the cottages, on to the road.

3. Turn right along the road and left at the sign for the Belas Knap ancient monument, and follow the path up through woodland.

4. In the field at the top follow the left-hand boundary (turning right at the corner), and enter the next field above. Keep to the left to reach the enclosure of the long barrow.

5. Leave the barrow by a stile and keep the hedge on your right. At a track turn left to reach a junction at Wontley Farm.

ABOVE AND TO THE right of Wadfield Farm lie the remains of Wadfield Roman villa. (It is not on the public right of way and not open to the public.) The site — on a slope above a valley with a plentiful water supply — is typical of many chosen by the Romans for their residences. Wadfield means 'woad field', suggesting that woad, the plant that produces blue dye, grew here at one time.

Belas Knap, a Neolithic long barrow of some importance, is an excellent example of a false-portal barrow. The Way passes the false portal, at the northern end of the mound, which was reconstructed 60 years ago to represent its appearance some 2,500 years earlier. Human bones were found in the chambers and behind the false entrance in the mid-19th century and the late 1920s, but generally the results of excavations have been disappointing. Some finds, however, can be seen in the Cheltenham Art Gallery and Museum and some in the Winchcombe Museum (see page 28), where there are also exhibits from the Wadfield villa.

The windswept plateau of Cleeve Hill

CLEEVE COMMON is managed by a Board of Conservators set up in 1891 following an act of Parliament and byelaws are displayed at the major entrances. The area consists of 2 square miles (5sq km) of limestone grassland which have been designated a Site of Special Scientific Interest. The remotest part of Cleeve Common lies between Wontley and the Washpool, and along here the Way gives a good view of the old quarry workings which provided stone for many of Cheltenham's buildings. The River Isbourne rises above the Washpool, where there are the remains of a sheep dip. The trig point near the topograph marks the second highest point of the Cotswolds, slightly lower than the true summit (1,083ft, 330m) which lies further back and, strangely, has no view.

ROUTE DIRECTIONS

1. Turn right at Wontley Farm to reach Cleeve Common. The Way over the common is marked with posts and the route may be subject to change from time to time.

2. From the gate go forward and turn right towards the northern boundary wall. The path bears left then right to reach a valley. Follow the valley downstream to the Washpool and bear left.

3. Follow the waymarks over the ridge, and descend to the quarry above the golf clubhouse, which is open for refreshment.

4. At the left-hand side of the quarry (used as a car park) turn left to follow the route just below the scarp edge, eventually turning left to reach a topograph and an Ordnance Survey trig point.

5. Follow the Way along the scarp edge, bearing left through the ramparts of the hillfort. Leave the common by Wheeler's Gate.

CLEEVE COMMON

WILDLIFE

Beech trees coming into full leaf

The Cotswolds is hardly the place to look for wild country, desolate moors and blasted heaths, for it has been cultivated for centuries. All the same, it supports an enjoyable range of thoroughly English wildlife.

The noble beechwoods of the Cotswold scarp and its valleys are at their richest in the Painswick area. Dark and mysterious, they glow green where sunlight pierces through to the leaves in spring and summer, and dapples the woodland floor. Deep leaf litter means that not many plants grow on the floor, but dog's mercury and birdsnest orchid can be found. The grotesque lobster moth caterpillar lives on beech trees and birds include the wood warbler. The beech groves are at their loveliest in the autumn, when the leaves turn to red and copper and gold.

There is a much greater variety of trees in the dip slope woods – ash and birch, oak and sycamore and yew. More light penetrates the tree cover, allowing a rich tangle of shrubs to thrive, including dogwood, hazel, privet, wild roses and brambles. In the spring and summer there are bluebells, violets, lily of the valley, deadly nightshade. Foxes, badgers and grey squirrels have their earths, setts and dreys – the last red squirrels had gone by 1950. There are fallow deer in some of the woods, and smaller numbers of roe deer and muntjac.

Up on the high downs at Rodborough and Minchinhampton Commons, Cleeve Cloud or Painswick Beacon, lime-loving wildflowers grow on grassy slopes nibbled by sheep and rabbits for centuries – pasque-flower and clustered bellflower, cowslip and numerous wild orchids, with giant thistles and milkwort in purple and mauve.

Along the hedgerows and roadside verges in spring and summer grow cow-parsley and celandine, scabious and

A foraging badger cub

Green woodpecker

meadow cranesbill. Hedges and drystone walls provide nesting places for robins, wrens and other birds. Kestrels nest in hedgerow trees and barn owls go hunting in the gloaming.

Snails are common in the Cotswolds because the limestone provides material for their shells. It is said that edible snails can still be found in the woods near Chedworth Roman Villa. They were introduced by the Romans, along with house mice and pheasants. Cotswolds butterflies and moths include painted lady, red admiral, clouded yellow, humming bird hawkmoth. The rufous grasshopper likes the limestone and so does the adonis blue butterfly.

Down in the Vale at Badegworth, between Cheltenham and Gloucester, is something unusual – a very rare type of marsh buttercup protected in a tiny reserve. You are not allowed inside, but in June and July you can admire the flowers from a gate.

Clouded yellow butterfly
Cowslips, found on meadows and grassland

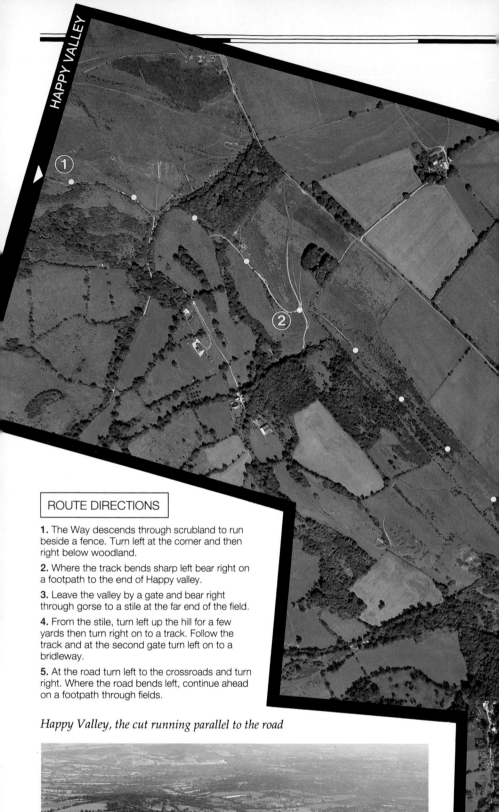

ROUTE DIRECTIONS

1. The Way descends through scrubland to run beside a fence. Turn left at the corner and then right below woodland.

2. Where the track bends sharp left bear right on a footpath to the end of Happy valley.

3. Leave the valley by a gate and bear right through gorse to a stile at the far end of the field.

4. From the stile, turn left up the hill for a few yards then turn right on to a track. Follow the track and at the second gate turn left on to a bridleway.

5. At the road turn left to the crossroads and turn right. Where the road bends left, continue ahead on a footpath through fields.

Happy Valley, the cut running parallel to the road

Cleeve Common to Leckhampton Hill 11½ miles (18.5km)

The Way follows the escarpment as it curves round Cheltenham, cradled in an amphitheatre of hills. Buses link the Way with Cheltenham from the A40 at Dowdeswell, the A435 at Seven Springs and below the Devil's Chimney at Leckhampton Hill. Views stretch across to Wales.

THE SCRUBLAND TYPICAL of the common continues southwards and characteristic limestone grassland flora such as knapweeds, kidney vetch, blue harebells and ox-eye daisies brightens the landscape during the summer.

Cattle and sheep graze freely on the common as they have done since medieval times when people living close by an area of open land had 'rights in common' with the owner. These rights included putting livestock out to graze, collecting turf or firewood, or fishing.

All commons were registered in the 1960s and anybody can find out the commoners' entitlements.

Happy valley is one of the many dry valleys in the Cotswolds that were probably eroded by the meltwaters flowing from ice caps situated on the uplands during the Ice Age. These powerful watercourses formed valleys above the main stream-bearing valleys which, watered by springs, continued to flow and have progressively deepened since the ice disappeared, leaving the dry tributary valleys 'hanging' above the main stream. Similar formations occur just north of Broadway Tower and further south at Crickley Hill.

THE LAND ABOVE Dowdeswell Reservoir is managed by the Gloucestershire Trust for Nature Conservation as a nature reserve. In spring the waterline is graced by rhododendrons in flower, and deer can be seen drinking of an early morning.

Unfortunately trunk roads and natterjack toads are not a happy combination and as, in the breeding season, the toads need to cross the A40 to reach the reservoir, do not be surprised to see road signs advising motorists to take care and even dedicated volunteers standing by ready to give a toad a lift across in a bucket! Since the 1981 Wildlife and Countryside Act a number of species gained special protection and natterjack toads are among the reptiles and amphibians it is illegal to catch, injure or kill. Some mammals, such as bats and otters, have total protection and it is even illegal to damage their homes or prevent them gaining access to their homes, whereas other mammals, such as badgers, have partial protection which makes it illegal to kill or injure them, or be in possession of a live or recently killed animal. Over 60 species of plants are listed as being illegal to pick, and it is illegal to dig up any wild plant unless you have the permission of the landowner.

A bus can be taken from the A40 into Cheltenham where there are many attractions. Not least of these is the excellent range of smart shops, numerous pubs and restaurants, or merely the opportunity to take a stroll around the streets to admire the classic Regency architecture (see page 42).

(see page 42).

ROUTE DIRECTIONS

1. Continue ahead through fields to cross a road. Follow the field boundary and, where the hedge turns right, bear left across the field to a stile.

2. Cross the stile, the farm track and another stile. Follow the path through the trees and, initially keeping to the left, descend through woodland.

3. Follow the fence of Dowdeswell Wood and cross the bridge over the reservoir slipway. Turn right and right again to reach the road near the Reservoir Inn.

4. Turn left along the A40 and cross to the signposted path on the other side. Take care; the traffic travels very fast along here.

5. Follow the path over the old railway trackbed which ran between Cheltenham and Banbury in Oxfordshire before becoming a casualty in the Beeching reorganisation, and continue with the hedge on your left towards Lineover Wood.

Dowdeswell Reservoir

DOWDESWELL

CHELTENHAM

Cheltenham's outdated image as a town populated by dyspeptic Anglo-Indian colonel's dates back to its days as a spa in the Regency period. The great Duke of Wellington came to take the waters in 1816 and his example attracted retired army officers with liver conditions who, like him, had served in India.

Cheltenham had been nothing more than a minor market town a hundred years before, when a medicinal spring was discovered. A spa developed in the 1730s, but it was a long visit by George III in 1788 which put the spa on the map. The population ballooned and speculators moved in to build today's delightful Regency town, with its Greek Revival terraces and crescents set along broad, tree-lined avenues. The houses were built of brick, but were given the Cotswold stone fronts and lacy cast-iron balconies and verandas. In the 1820s a self-made businessman named Joseph Pitt developed the suburb of Pittsville and built its grandly domed Pump Room, modelled on a temple in Athens.

In the heart of the town Montpellier Walk leads from the Rotunda past shops separated by Greek-style statues to the Promenade and Imperial Square, one of the noblest townscapes in Britain.

One of the few pre-Regency buildings is the parish church, St Mary's, though even it owes much to 19th-century restoration. The stained glass is Victorian, including the popular *Last Supper* window in the south aisle.

Not far away in Clarence Street, the Art Gallery and Museum has a notable collection of Arts and Crafts Movement furniture by the 'Cotswold School' of designers – C.R. Ashbee, Ernest Gimson,

C.F.A Voysey, Gordon Russell and others – as well as jewellery, metalwork and ceramics. There are English and Dutch paintings to enjoy, too, and material on the Cotswolds rural life, local history and archaeology.

Gustav Holst, the composer of *The Planets*, was born in a typical Regency house in Clarence Road in 1874. The family was of Swedish extraction and

Elegant houses with cast-iron balconies in Imperial Square

his father was a music teacher in the town. The house is a museum to the composer, with photographs, musical instruments and mementos, period rooms and a Victorian kitchen and laundry.

Cheltenham is known for its schools, theatres and smart shops. Lively events every year include a music festival in July and literature festival in October, but the liveliest of all is the major steeplechase meeting at Cheltenham racecourse in March, when both the Gold Cup and the Champion Hurdle are run.

A fountain featuring Neptune being drawn by seahorses decorates the Promenade

Montpellier Walk, one of the town's most charming streets

LINEOVER WOOD, managed by the Woodland Trust, takes its name from 'lind ofer', meaning the lime-tree hill. The depression in the field just beyond the wood was caused by the excavation of stone used to build the A40. Until about 70 years ago all Cotswold roads were made of stone and resembled the tracks the Way followed south of Cleeve Common.

A shooting school has been set up in Chatcombe Wood, for which a part of the wood has been cleared near the bridleway the Way follows. The direction of fire is away from the path, however, and the launching point for the clay pigeons is positioned at the edge of the wood.

The Cotswolds supports a variety of woodland habitats and where there is a good mix of tree and shrub species birdlife can be particularly rich. During the spring songbirds fill the air with sound and winter visitors include flocks of brambling from Scandinavia.

Winter, for obvious reasons, is a good time to observe woodland birds and there is also the likelihood at this time of seeing birds more usually associated with open fields and hedgerows as the woods offer additional protection and food sources.

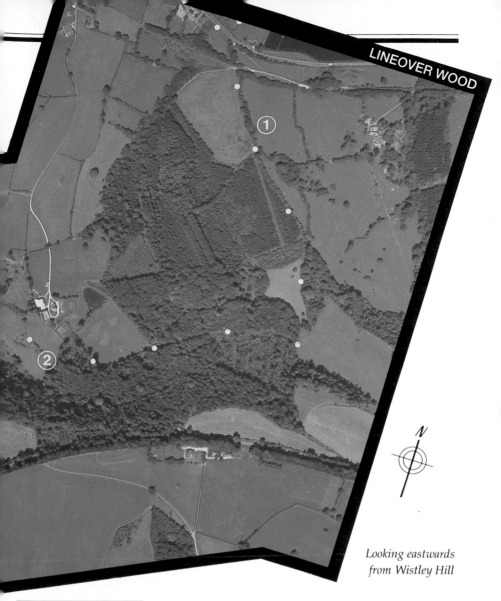

Looking eastwards from Wistley Hill

ROUTE DIRECTIONS

1. Follow the Way uphill beside Lineover Wood and turn right into the heart of the woodland near the top.

2. Cross the next field, pass the remains of a small quarry, and continue up the steep side of Ravensgate Common, from which there is a fine view to the north of the east side of Cheltenham.

3. At the top turn left through a belt of woodland and follow the track to the A436.

4. Here the official route turns right and follows the main road to the junction at Seven Springs. However, as this involves about a mile (1.6km) of main road walking, the walker may wish to take the following alternative which is about 2 miles (3.2km) long. Walkers opting to stay on the main road will pick up the route description at number 2 on page 46.

5. Alternative route: cross the A436 and enter Chatcombe Wood. Follow the bridleway through the wood and along the field boundary. Enter the next field on your left (near the line of pylons) and walk diagonally across.

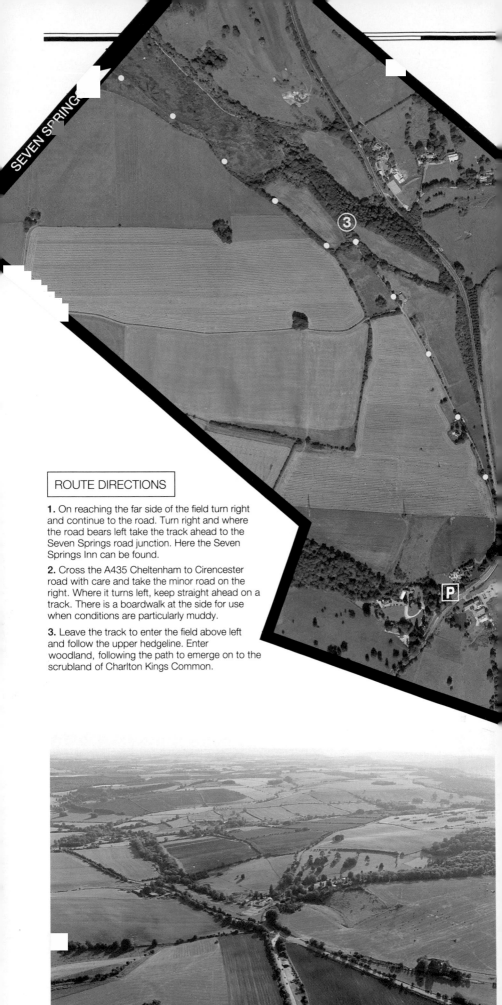

③

ROUTE DIRECTIONS

1. On reaching the far side of the field turn right and continue to the road. Turn right and where the road bears left take the track ahead to the Seven Springs road junction. Here the Seven Springs Inn can be found.

2. Cross the A435 Cheltenham to Cirencester road with care and take the minor road on the right. Where it turns left, keep straight ahead on a track. There is a boardwalk at the side for use when conditions are particularly muddy.

3. Leave the track to enter the field above left and follow the upper hedgeline. Enter woodland, following the path to emerge on to the scrubland of Charlton Kings Common.

AFTER CROSSING the Cheltenham to Cirencester road it is worth diverting left on to the A436 Gloucester road for a few yards to look at the Seven Springs by the parking area. The springs now run into a pool forming the source of the River Churn. The Churn, from which the names North and South Cerney and Cirencester are derived, flows on to join the Thames. Although the official source of the Thames is near Kemble, there are many who claim Seven Springs as the real source.

The track just before Charlton Kings Common can be very muddy in winter and the boardwalk at the side is an example of the kind of work done by the Cotswold Voluntary Warden Service. The Service was set up in 1968 and members of all ages and from all walks of life spend a total of approximately 28,000 working hours a year (equivalent to 16 full-time people) looking after an area of 800 square miles (2,071sq km). Wardens, identifiable by a green-and-yellow armband or badge, regularly patrol footpaths and country parks and are more than happy to provide visitors with help or information. Their work includes clearance, waymarking, stile and bridge building, maintaining drystone walls, tree planting and leading guided walks.

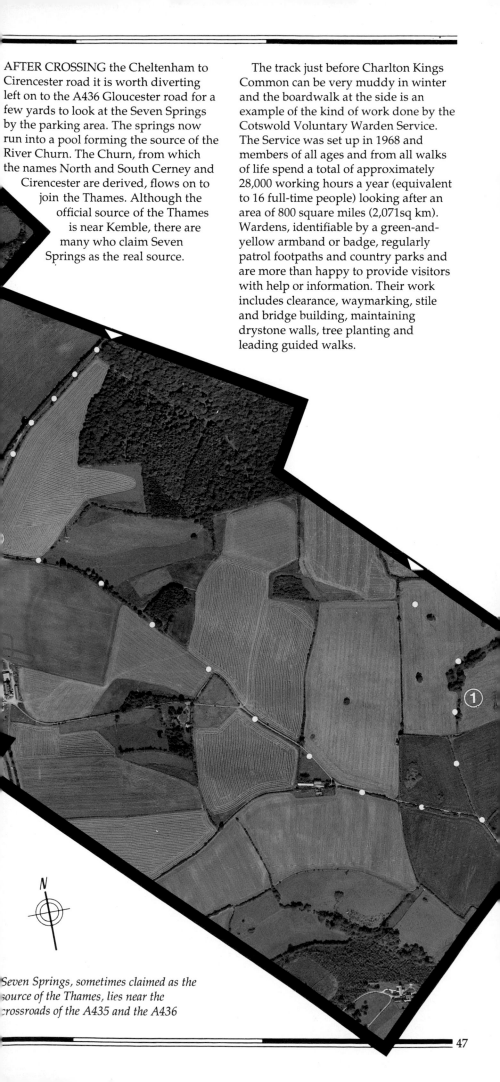

Seven Springs, sometimes claimed as the source of the Thames, lies near the crossroads of the A435 and the A436

CHARLTON KINGS COMMON and Leckhampton Hill impose a natural constraint on Cheltenham's development but this did not prevent developers in the last century wanting to build here on the slopes below the Way, which resulted in riots by local people. Today the area is managed as a Site of Special Scientific interest by Cheltenham Borough Council who ensure the preservation of its beauty.

Leckhampton Hill has been quarried extensively over the centuries, with output reaching its peak at the end of the 19th century when tramways were built to remove the stone, much of which can be seen in the terraces of Cheltenham.

The distinctive and much-photographed rock formation known as the Devil's Chimney is thought to be a relic of the quarrying. It is extremely unsafe and although it has often been climbed in the past, these days doing so is prohibited.

ROUTE DIRECTIONS

1. Follow the waymarks through the gorse keeping to the rim of the hill. The path bears west then south as Charlton Kings Common merges with Leckhampton Hill.

2. Continue to the topograph, which unfortunately is not orientated quite correctly. (A signposted detour can be taken from this point to the Devil's Chimney.) Continue to the top edge of Salterley

quarry, now used as a car park. Follow the path to the road.

3. Turn left up the hill and just before reaching a house on the left turn right and follow the track south towards Ullenwood, passing the golf course on the way. Star Centre, just past the golf course, helps those with severe handicaps to live their lives to a fuller extent than they may ever have dreamt possible.

4. At the road turn right to a crossroads and take the minor road opposite.

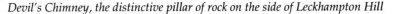

Devil's Chimney, the distinctive pillar of rock on the side of Leckhampton Hill

Crickley Hill

Leckhampton Hill to Fiddler's Elbow 10 miles (16km)

In this section the Way passes several ancient settlements and there is an opportunity to visit a Roman villa. Gloucester lies to the west of the route and can be reached most directly by road from Birdlip.

CRICKLEY HILL country park opened in 1979 and is managed by the Gloucestershire County Council, who owns it jointly with the National Trust. There is a visitor centre on the site, plus waymarked nature trails and displays relating to the history of the area.

The promontory of Crickley Hill was an important Iron Age fortification and at the entrance to the hillfort there is a viewpoint from which can be identified the Neolithic and Iron Age occupations that have been subject to annual excavations since 1969. Volunteers come from all over the world to assist with these excavations for about six weeks in July and August, and during an open weekend the finds can be inspected.

There is a causewayed enclosure dating from around 3000BC and the earthworks can be seen in the country park.

ROUTE DIRECTIONS

1. Follow the road, past an old camp on the left, to reach a strip of woodland on the left. At the far edge of this, turn left into the field. (Avoid the bridleway, which enters the woodland just before the path you require.)

2. Follow the scarp edge into another strip of woodland and at the far end bear left to enter Crickley Hill country park.

3. Pass the buildings on the left, which include toilets, to enter the hillfort. Bear right round the edge of the hill to a waymark post.

4. Turn sharp left and follow the wall on the right. The path veers into the woodland and after an open area the Way turns right on to a track at the far side of some cottages.

5. At the road cross to the Air Balloon Inn, which offers convenient refreshment, if in somewhat noisy surroundings, then walk beside the A417 Cirencester road on the upper side of the inn. Follow the footway which diverges from the road to the right on to Barrow Wake Common.

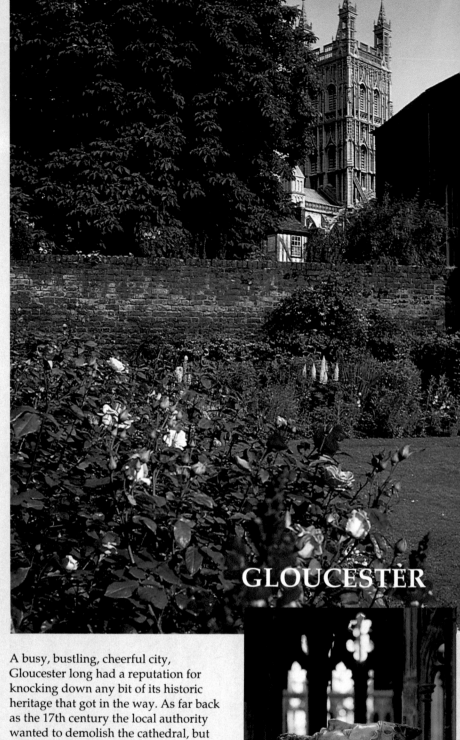

GLOUCESTER

A busy, bustling, cheerful city, Gloucester long had a reputation for knocking down any bit of its historic heritage that got in the way. As far back as the 17th century the local authority wanted to demolish the cathedral, but better sense and Oliver Cromwell fortunately prevailed. Recently, however, Gloucester's attitude to its past has changed and the city now has a powerful battery of tourist attractions.

Gloucester grew up as a Roman town round a legionary fort constructed in the 1st century at the lowest crossing of the River Severn. The centre of the city still has the basic Roman plan, with four main streets crossing in the middle. Remains of the Roman east gate and its successors are still visible. Roman sculptures and mosaics can be admired in the City Museum along with collections of barometers and 18th-century furniture, and an aquarium.

The tower of Gloucester cathedral. Treasures inside include the tomb of Edward II (inset), which is carved from alabaster, Purbeck marble and oolitic limestone

The docks, with the triple-masted Saraan

The cathedral, which is dominated by its spectacularly magnificent, amply pinnacled tower, is one of the buildings where the Perpendicular style of architecture first developed in the 14th century. It was then part of the Benedictine abbey of St Peter. When King Edward II was gruesomely murdered at nearby Berkeley Castle in 1327, the monks accepted his body for burial. Pilgrims came flocking to his tomb and the monks rebuilt their church on the profits.

The King's tomb is still seen near the high altar. The tremendous east window, the size of a tennis court, is the largest in the country and commemorates the battle of Crécy.

In a lane leading to the cathedral is a small Beatrix Potter shop and museum, in what is claimed to be the original of the Tailor of Gloucester's house. The enjoyable Folk Museum, in a row of half-timbered buildings in Westgate Street, has displays on local history, home life in the past and traditional Severn fishing for eels and elvers.

The Severn is a tricky, notoriously difficult river and in the 1820s the Gloucester merchants built a 16-mile (25.7km) ship canal from the city down to the Bristol Channel. The docks and warehouses have been splendidly refurbished and are now home to the National Waterways Museum, which tells the story of canals. In the Custom House is the museum of the Gloucestershire Regiment, the 'glorious Glosters'. Close by and on no account to be missed is the fabulous Robert Opie Collection of packages, containers and advertising – a profoundly nostalgic trip back to the day-before-yesterday's shopping.

BARROW WAKE has long provided a spectacular prospect over the Vale of Gloucester. Chosen Hill and Robinswood Hill, outliers of the escarpment, lie close to Gloucester itself and the whole view is framed by Crickley Hill on the right and by The Peak and Cooper's Hill on the left. In the old quarries here the famous Birdlip mirror was discovered among Iron Age remains. Made of bronze and finely engraved, it was found buried with a woman along with bronze bowls, a silver brooch and a decorated bucket. These treasures, which can now be seen in Gloucester City Museum, give some clue to the wealth of the *Dobunni* — the tribe who dominated the Cotwolds in the Iron Age.

The road striking south-east from Birdlip village across the vale below follows the line of the Roman Ermine Way from Cirencester (*Corinium*) to Gloucester (*Glevum*).

The woodlands of the Witcombe Estate consist of a good mixture of species with stands of conifer providing a contrast to beech, ash and sycamore. This method of mixed planting enables the faster-growing conifer to act as a 'nurse' to the beech and, when extracted, leaves a maturing deciduous woodland. Below the canopy wild raspberry and strawberry can be found, as can deadly nightshade, and care should be taken that young children are not tempted by the poisonous shiny black berries. There are pheasant-rearing areas along the route through the wood and dogs should be kept under close control. Sometimes the 'kia kia' call of the buzzard is heard.

Birdlip village above Birdlip Hill, one of the steepest descents to the Vale of Gloucester

ROUTE DIRECTIONS

1. Follow the waymarks across the common, keeping height. Another topograph lies above the path.

2. At the far end cross a stile to walk at the edge of the field and continue into woodland.

3. Bear right to visit The Peak. Retrace your steps and bear right through woodland and old quarries to reach the road. (To reach Birdlip and the Royal George turn left.)

4. Cross the road, taking the footpath leading right, downhill. Turn sharp left to follow a track into Witcombe Wood.

GREAT WITCOMBE ROMAN VILLA was built around three sides of a courtyard overlooking the valley. The remains are now cared for by English Heritage, and are open at any reasonable time.

Each year, on Spring bank holiday Monday, the cheese-rolling ceremony for which Cooper's Hill is famous takes place. Proceedings take the form of four races in which the contestants chase a Double Gloucester cheese down the slope. The official lets the cheese go on a count of three, the participants start on four – and an ambulance waits tucked out of sight at the bottom!

Cooper's Hill, bought in the 1960s by Gloucestershire County Council to prevent further quarrying, is now a Local Nature Reserve. The Reserve is divided into two parts and the Way passes from one to the other between two meadows preserved as a grassland nature reserve by the Gloucestershire Trust for Nature Conservation.

Beyond Cooper's Hill the Way enters Buckholt Wood, which is a National Nature Reserve managed by English Nature.

ROUTE DIRECTIONS

1. Continue on the contour through the wood. (A branching path descends to Great Witcombe Roman villa on the right.)

2. Follow the road into Cooper's Hill village, passing the welcome Haven Tea Garden on the right.

3. At the foot of the steep slope on the left (where the cheese-rolling ceremony takes place), bear left behind the house and enter the wood. Turn left and left again to emerge on to a steep grassy slope.

4. Turn right at the maypole to re-enter the

woodland on the right-hand path. At a track junction, follow the lower track to the left. Just before the open field ahead turn right on a path between two fields. Turn left, following the Way as it descends to another track. Bear left and follow the path as it bears right. (The steep stepped path leaving the Way on the right leads to the Fiddler's Elbow picnic area, toilets and occasionally present mobile snack bar).

5. The Way leads up through woodland to a road. Turn right and cross to the junction with the A46 Cheltenham to Stroud road. Cross to the footway opposite and turn left to enter Buckholt Wood. (Walkers wishing to visit Prinknash Abbey (see page 61) should turn right along the footway).

Wooded Cooper's Hill, south of Brockworth

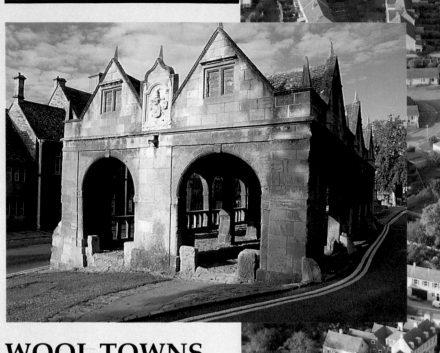

WOOL TOWNS AND MARKET TOWNS

A line of historic towns lies close to the floor of the Cotswolds edge. The queen of them is generally agreed to be Chipping Campden. Its wide, gracefully curving main street is lined with stone houses which are a living museum of the Cotswolds style of domestic architecture from the 14th century to the 20th. Chipping means 'market' and a weekly market has been held here since at least the 13th century. The soaring church of St James the Great testifies to the wealth of the town's wool merchants, whose brasses and memorials lie inside. It has been a centre for crafts ever since 1902, when C.R. Ashbee moved his Guild of Handicrafts here from London.

Winchcombe is another former wool town with a fine Perpendicular church. Little is left of the rich Benedictine abbey which once dominated it and built the George Hotel for pilgrims.

Painswick is a jewel, full of charming stone houses and cottages, narrow lanes and flourishing antiques and crafts shops. St Mary's Church with its slender spire is surrounded by one of the most fascinating churchyards in England. It has an amazing collection of 17th-and 18th-century stone tombs, richly decorated by local masons with carved scrolls, shells, flowers and foliage, cherubs and skulls with bats wings and teeth.

Stroud and Dursley, once mill towns, live by light industry now. The local

*Classic Cotswold architecture in Painswick
Inset: Chipping Campden's market hall*

history can be followed up in Stroud's District Museum. Stroud's railway station was designed by the great Isambard Kingdom Brunel and the canal through the Golden valley was built in the 1780s to link the Severn with the Thames.

Wotton-under-Edge, whose name neatly describes its dramatic situation, is a pleasant market town with charming old inns. The Ram Inn of 1350 is possibly the oldest house in Wotton. The church has an impressive

Wares for sale in The Shambles, Stroud

Perpendicular tower and inside is the sumptuous 14th-century brass of Lord and Lady Berkeley: at her feet is a little dog with a collar of bells. Isaac Pitman was living in Orchard Street when he devised his new system of shorthand in the 1830s, and there's a plaque on the house.

Further south, Chipping Sodbury is another attractive market town with a broad main street and an imposing church. In its humbler way, it makes a suitable counterpoint to Chipping Campden at the other end of the line.

Fiddler's Elbow (A46) to Standish Woods 8½ miles (13.5km)

The highlight of this stretch is arriving at the lovely town of Painswick with its famous churchyard and handsome grey-stone buildings. Beyond, more spectacular views — from the hillfort on Haresfield Beacon in particular — await the walker.

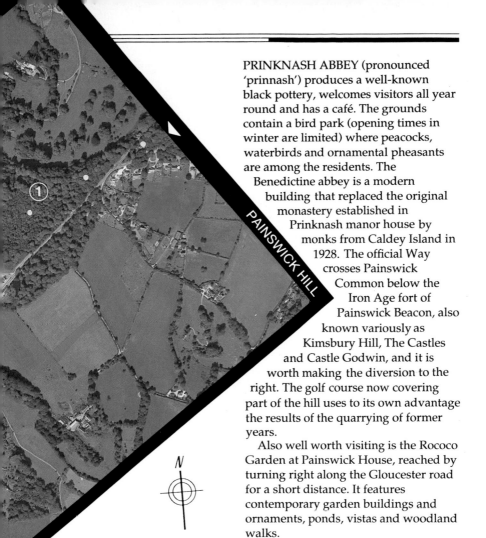

PRINKNASH ABBEY (pronounced 'prinnash') produces a well-known black pottery, welcomes visitors all year round and has a café. The grounds contain a bird park (opening times in winter are limited) where peacocks, waterbirds and ornamental pheasants are among the residents. The Benedictine abbey is a modern building that replaced the original monastery established in Prinknash manor house by monks from Caldey Island in 1928. The official Way crosses Painswick Common below the Iron Age fort of Painswick Beacon, also known variously as Kimsbury Hill, The Castles and Castle Godwin, and it is worth making the diversion to the right. The golf course now covering part of the hill uses to its own advantage the results of the quarrying of former years.

Also well worth visiting is the Rococo Garden at Painswick House, reached by turning right along the Gloucester road for a short distance. It features contemporary garden buildings and ornaments, ponds, vistas and woodland walks.

ROUTE DIRECTIONS

1. The path through Buckholt Wood crosses a road and converges on a track coming from the Royal William Inn on the left.

2. Follow the road past Castle Lodge to take a grassy track crossing Painswick Common. Follow this across the golf course to another road. (A diversion to the right leads to the Ordnance Survey trig point on Painswick Beacon returning to the same road.) Turn left then right to follow a track leading to Catsbrain quarry. Before reaching the quarry entrance, bear left on a path leading through woodland to an open grassy slope.

3. Cross this open area to the right-hand side of the cemetery wall ahead. Follow the path with the upper wall on your left. Cross the golf course into woodland and continue to a road which leads to a junction with the Gloucester to Painswick road, beside the Glyde Orphanage.

The interior of Painswick hillfort has suffered from quarrying over the years

ROUTE DIRECTIONS

1. At the Gloucester to Painswick road turn left then continue ahead down Gloucester Street into Painswick. Turn right into New Street. At the end of the churchyard turn right into Edge Lane. Turn left into Hambutts field, where camping is allowed courtesy of the Open Spaces Society. Keep the hedge on the left, and just beyond the drive turn left, between gardens, to a field.

2. Follow the marked path ahead to a stile. Beyond the stile the path follows the left-hand hedge to a junction. Here bear right diagonally across the field to a target disc.

3. Keep the hedge on your right and descend to Washbrook Farm. Continue ahead to a track which turns left.

4. Part way up the field bear left over a stile. Walk towards the woodland and follow the path to a footbridge, then bear left to a stile and turn sharp left to reach a stone squeeze-stile on to the road. Turn right to the Gloucester to Stroud road and the Edgemoor Inn.

5. Cross the road and take the path ahead, turning right to a waymark directing diagonally left up Rudge Hill.

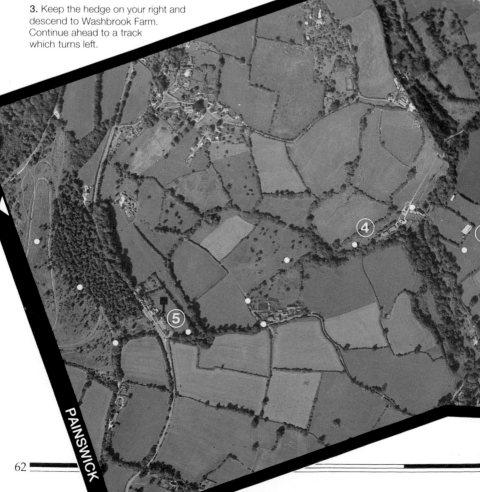

PAINSWICK

PAINSWICK, SOMETIMES CALLED 'the Queen of the Cotswolds', is characterised by a greyer stone than is found further north. The town is well worth exploring and there are a number of good pubs and places to stay. A tourist information centre can be found in the library.

The churchyard features a fine collection of table top tombs and, if time permits, count the yew trees. Legend has it that only 99 will grow, with either a newcomer appearing or an old one dying to maintain the number.

Each 19 September (or the Sunday after it) the 'clipping' ceremony takes place in the churchyard. This clipping has nothing to do with trimming the yews, but is derived from 'ycleping', an Old English word meaning embracing, and during the ceremony children clasp hands as they encircle Mother Church.

Painswick's wealth came from cloth-making and a number of mills were built along the Painswick Stream for this purpose. The mills are now converted to private dwellings but the teasel plants growing locally are descendants of those whose dead flowerheads were used to raise the nap on the cloth.

St Mary's Church in the middle of Painswick

MUCH OF THE ROUTE between Stockend Wood and the Stroud valley lies in the care of the National Trust, and the topograph south of the Cripplegate car park shows the extent of the Trust property in relief. In many places sympathetic landowners with property adjoining land belonging to the Trust have agreed, under covenant, to keep their land in its current use. Much of the land in the valley below is protected in this way.

Included in the Trust estate here is Haresfield Beacon, one of the spurs projecting from the main scarp towards the Severn Vale. As with many of these spurs, prehistoric man chose Haresfield as a defensive site because of the natural protection afforded by the promontory. Nowadays the Beacon is most appreciated for the tremendous views it commands, with the Forest of Dean visible beyond the loop of the Severn.

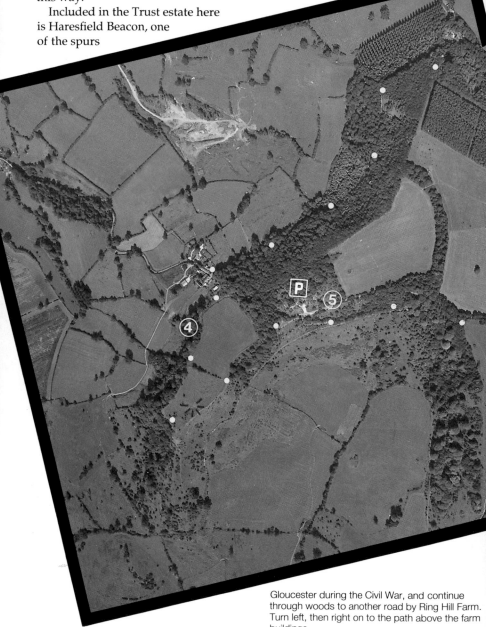

ROUTE DIRECTIONS

1. From the top of Rudge Hill follow the path through the old quarry area to the Edge to Randwick road.

2. Cross the road and enter Stockend Wood, bearing left downhill to meet a track. Turn left and continue to another road, rather charmingly called Pound of Candles Lane. Turn right to Cliffwell House.

3. Turn left, pass the Siege Stone which commemorates the raising of the siege of Gloucester during the Civil War, and continue through woods to another road by Ring Hill Farm. Turn left, then right on to the path above the farm buildings.

4. The path rises (ignore the gate on the left) to a stile. Continue ahead to the Ordnance Survey trig point on Haresfield Beacon. Return to the main scarp on the path facing south, encountering a stile and gate before the car-parking area.

5. At the National Trust cairn turn right down the steps and left beside a wall. This path joins a track. Bear left to rise through a copse to an open field.

6. Bear right along the ridge to the topograph. Return to the main scarp and the car park at Cripplegate, leaving it by a squeeze-stile to follow the upper path into Standish Woods.

HARESFIELD HILL

QUARRYING AND INDUSTRY

The scars of quarrying on Cleeve Common

Genuine quarried Cotswold stone is a valuable commodity these days

Anyone exploring the Cotswolds will soon come across disused quarries, most of them quite small, long abandoned and overgrown now with grass, ivy and a tangle of blackberry bushes. Many towns and villages had their own, and villagers had the right to cut stone from their parish quarry. Most of the houses in Chipping Campden today were built of stone from the Westington Quarry above the town. Leckhampton Quarry, where the Devil's Chimney is a celebrated curiosity, provided the stone for the smart Regency terraces of Cheltenham. Old workings can be found on Minchinhampton Common, at Rodborough Common, near the picnic site at Coaley Peak, at the Fish Hill picnic site above Broadway and in many other locations.

The quarrymen in the old days used simple picks and crowbars, axes, wedges, hoists and cranes, and cut the stone with a saw as easily as if it was wood. Stone for roofing was left out to spend the winter under wet sacks. Water froze in the cracks in the stone and when the thaw came, the stone would split along the cracks, into tiles. The few Cotswolds quarries open today operate on a much bigger scale, with explosives and mechanical diggers, and the stone is made into cement and artificial compounds.

The major Cotswolds industry down into the 19th century was the manufacture of cloth, which was done at home. The women and girls did the spinning (hence 'spinster' for an unmarried girl) and the men the weaving. Many of the older houses in places like Painswick were once the homes and workshops of weavers.

The invention of improved spinning and weaving machinery in the 18th century put paid to this cottage industry and spawned the modern factory. Handsome stone mills can still be seen in the Stroud area of the southern Cotswolds, where they spread along the River Frome in the Golden valley and beside its tributaries, using the water to provide power. Stroud was a busy industrial centre for a time, making scarlet coats for soldiers and huntsmen, but the industry moved away to the North of England.

A few of the old mills are still working, such as the impressive one at King's Stanley, built in 1813, five storeys of stone and brick on a cast-iron frame and claimed as the first fireproof building in England. Others have been turned into flats and stand as reminders of a vanished age.

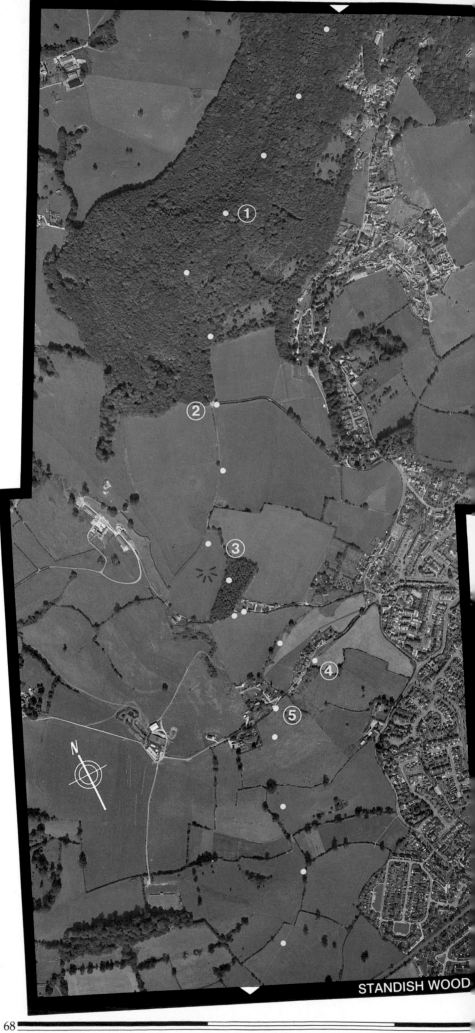

STANDISH WOOD

Standish Woods to Dursley

11 miles (17.5km)

The Way crosses the industrialised Stroud valleys before making its way past two famous long barrows. Buses can be taken into Stroud from Ryeford, and from Stroud connections can be made to Gloucester (see page 52) some 10 miles (16km) away. Stonehouse station is connected to the Way by a footpath which follows the railway track westwards.

THE EXTENT OF the Stroud valley opens up on the descent from Standish Woods. Stroud grew up at the confluence of several rivers and the main routes to the town follow the valleys: the Painswick Stream accompanies the road from Cheltenham to the north-east; the Slad valley road is now part of a modern Scenic Route from the High Wold, also to the north-east; the road from Cirencester, the River Frome and the Stroudwater Canal run along the Golden valley to the east; and the road from Bath lies in the Nailsworth valley to the south. At one time all these valleys had mills built along the floor, and some remain as magnificent examples of industrial architecture. Many, fortunately, have been rescued from dereliction and are being used for other purposes, such as apartments or restaurants.

ROUTE DIRECTIONS

1. The Way is marked through Standish Woods but take care to avoid other paths marked with a yellow spot, denoting a local route. Follow the Way's white spot, bearing right on the wooded ridge. During the descent there is a notice advising of a National Trust campsite to the left.

2. The path emerges at a lane. Cross this and walk down the field to a gate. Just below the end of the field boundary on your left is a gate in the right-hand wall. At this point strike left across the open field to a stile.

3. Beyond the stile the path leads down through the trees of Maiden Hill to a road. Turn left for a few yards then turn right and follow the path across the field. Cross the next stile and walk straight down across the field to an alleyway.

4. Turn right along the road, ignore the first stile on the left and proceed to another on the left, opposite cottages.

5. Continue down to a stile by a gateway, where the ground can be very boggy in rainy periods.

Haresfield Beacon, a promontory with superb views

In the early 19th century King's Stanley, south-east of Stroud, possesed the largest cloth mill in the Stroud valley

THE DESCENT TO the Frome valley provides a good view of stone-built Ebley Mill, recently refurbished and now used to house the offices of Stroud District Council.

Just after leaving the A419 the Way crosses the Stroudwater Canal, disused but still containing water. Further west the construction of the M5 and its A419 link has obliterated it.

The canal was opened in 1779 to link Stroud with the navigable River Severn 8 miles (12.8km) away at Upper Framilode but the scheme was never very successful, and the problem of retaining the water through the porous Cotswold stone, combined with competition from the infant railways, led to its demise. Restored in the early part of this century by the County Council, the canal was finally abandoned in the 1930s. A Trust has funded repairs and parts of it again hold water, but so much of it has been built over that it is unlikely ever to be re-opened along the whole of its length.

Stroud, lacking the architectural charm of Cheltenham or Painswick, has remained refreshingly workmanlike and untouristy — quite a rarity in the Cotswolds. Local history can be discovered in the district museum in Lansdown; there is an open-air market; and just outside the town there is a sports and leisure centre.

ROUTE DIRECTIONS

1. Continue up the field and at the gate bear right to follow the hedge on your left. In the third field bear left downhill to the footbridge over the Stroud to Gloucester railway. (There is a footpath to Stonehouse station along the north side of the track.)

2. Beyond the bridge follow the right-hand hedge to an alleyway leading on to the A419. (Buses can be taken from here into Stroud.) Turn right, under a footbridge, to a junction and turn left towards King's Stanley.

3. Beyond the mill building on the right, turn left into a field and follow the path above the new housing in King's Stanley. At the end of the next field cross the stile to the right of the track.

4. Keep to the right of the farm buildings, cross two stiles, and bear left to the access road for the farm.

5. Cross into a field and bear right under power lines to cross a stile. Keep the hedge on your right. Beyond the next stile bear slightly left and continue beside gardens to reach the road by King's Stanley Baptist Church. Bear left on the footway and cross into Coombe Lane on the right.

LOOKING BACK FROM the pasture the view takes in the village of Selsley and its unusual church tower, with Selsley Common above it to the right.

There is a great mix of woodland on this stretch of the route. Much of it is now owned by the Woodland Trust who are committed to maintaining and creating woodlands, and managing them commercially in order to help finance conservation schemes. The number of plaques passed on the route indicates the high level of public support the Trust receives.

The Way between here and Uleybury is very easy to walk these days, largely due to the work of volunteers and those on government employment schemes. Note the long stretches of revetting supporting the path.

In places the results of the gales of recent years can be seen. The most notable casualties have been beech trees with their shallow root system. Beneath the trees there is a plentiful understorey of shrubs, and an abundance of ivy (some of it obscuring waymarks). In spring plants such as dog's mercury and bluebells are abundant.

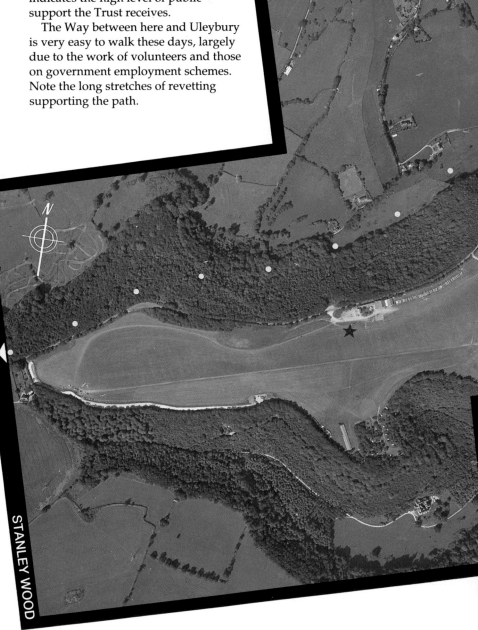

STANLEY WOOD

ROUTE DIRECTIONS

1. Where the farm entry turns left, bear right on to a rough lane. Continue ahead up a narrow enclosed path, over a stile and across pasture to a lane.

2. Turn left, then left again along a track into Penn Wood. Take the right-hand path and follow the contour in the same general direction, ignoring paths joining it and steps on the left.

3. The path emerges at a field above Woodside Farm. Stay on the same level and re-enter the woodland beyond.

Selsey, looking towards Stanley Wood

COTSWOLD STONE

The work of man has blended in admirably with the operations of nature in the Cotwolds because the limestone of the hills is excellent building stone and easily quarried. Used not only for houses and churches, but for barns, stiles and field walls, it ranges in colour from a creamy white through varying shades of pale gold, mellow honey and yellow-brown to pale grey.

The stone is called oolite, from the Greek words for 'egg' and 'stone' because it is composed of small rounded globules, like the roe of a fish. When first cut from the quarry, it is soft enough to be easily chiselled or cut with a saw, but it hardens on exposure to the air to create a strong, smooth surface. Since it could be split easily it was used for roofs as well as walls, but the tiles were thick and heavy, and when the thinner Welsh slates became readily available in the 19th century, local stone was less used for roofing.

The drystone walls which are an attractive feature of the landscape were

Ornate gabling on Stanway House

usually made with stones from the top layer of limestone, dug from a pit on each farm. A wall of this kind is built without mortar by skilful fitting together of stones of varying size, shape and weight. A well-built one will hold together even if the foundation sinks. The craft goes back to prehistoric times, but most of the walls today date from the 18th century and later, after the enclosure of the old open fields.

Stone for building houses has to be quarried from deeper layers and most Cotswold villages once had their own quarry. The hue of the stone varies slightly from one quarry and village to another.

The Cotswolds local style of architecture can be seen at its best in villages like Snowshill and Stanton, and towns like Chipping Campden and Painswick. Gables are a dominant feature. Often there are many of them and they rise as high as the ridge of the steeply pitched roof. Above are tall chimney stacks and below are long ranges of smallish windows. It is fundamentally a plain, simple style, but the fact that the stone was easy to work allowed for graceful nuances in the way of ornamental finials, grand doorways or stones inscribed with dates, initials or coats of arms. Combining simplicity with elegance, it is an architecture of enduring charm.

Sturdy manor houses (above) typify Cotswold building — as do the cottages in villages such as Snowshill (below)

Uleybury, a classic hillfort with its flat top and steep sides, was occupied during the Iron Age by the Dobunni *tribe*

ROUTE DIRECTIONS

1. Continue through the wood, finally bearing left round the rim of an old quarry to the Coaley Peak picnic site, where there are toilets.

2. Cross the picnic area to the Nympsfield long barrow. Continue through a gate, bearing right to the scarp edge. After another gate, follow the path to the topograph.

COALEY PEAK

3. Follow the path bearing right below the old quarries into woodland, and continue to the road. Cross the road and follow it uphill. At the junction bear right on to the slip road. To visit Hetty Pegler's Tump continue along the road for ½ mile (800m). To enter the long barrow — take a torch — continue ahead to Crawley Barns to obtain a key. After returning the key to Crawley Barns continue along the road to rejoin the Way at 5, below.)

4. Turn right down a bridleway (Knapp Lane) and, before the cottages, turn left. Ignore the bridleway to the right and shortly reach a cross-track. Cross this and climb the steps to continue through the woodland to rejoin the bridleway below Crawley Barns.

5. Almost immediately a path junction is reached, close to the road. (An optional extra of just over a mile (1.6km) is afforded by taking the footpath to the ramparts of the Uleybury hillfort.) The Way itself takes the bridleway to the right below the ramparts.

COALEY PEAK PICNIC site was opened in 1976 on farmland acquired for the purpose. The grass-mix sown was intended to represent typical traditional Cotswold meadowland, and the pink blush of sainfoin in spring is a delight to the eye. Nature trails weave through the woodland of Frocester Hill below.

Cotswold Voluntary Wardens planted the strip of trees beside the road at the picnic site and were accused of 'drawing the curtain' on the view by a lady who took coaches of the elderly and infirm to enjoy that particular view from the road! However, the magnificent sight of the great bends of the River Severn can be enjoyed from the picnic tables – also provided by the Warden Service from public donations.

Nympsfield village, east of the scarp edge, gives its name to the long barrow near the picnic site. This chambered burial mound is smaller than Hetty Pegler's Tump, also known as Uley long barrow, which has five chambers, although only three can be visited for safety reasons. Both barrows are in the care of English Heritage.

The National Trust owns the property around the topograph, from where there is a good view of the hilly walk ahead. Between here and Stinchcombe Hill, above Dursley, the walker climbs 1,000ft (305m).

CAM LONG DOWN, like similar features in Britain, has a story to explain its origin: the Devil, irritated because the good people of Gloucestershire built so many fine churches, decided to drown them by damming the River Severn. He filled his barrow with rocks and set off. Tiring, he met a cobbler with strings of boots and shoes round his neck, and enquired how far it was to the Severn. The quick-witted cobbler, sensing something unpleasant, said 'Look how many boots I have worn out coming from the Severn'. Whereupon the Devil gave up, emptied his barrow and so created Cam Long Down! There are other local names for this outlier on the scarp edge. One, the Dough Trough, likens it to an upturned loaf of bread.

Like other towns the Way has passed, Dursley prospered from the cloth trade. Although the Market House dates from those times, there are few other buildings which pre-date the 19th century. One which does, the church of St James, lost its spire in the 17th century and never had it replaced. When the cloth industry declined, new vigour was brought to the town in the mid-19th century by the establishment of Listers, an engineering firm specialising in diesel engines.

For walkers, Dursley is a useful place to stop as it has accommodation and several places to eat and drink.

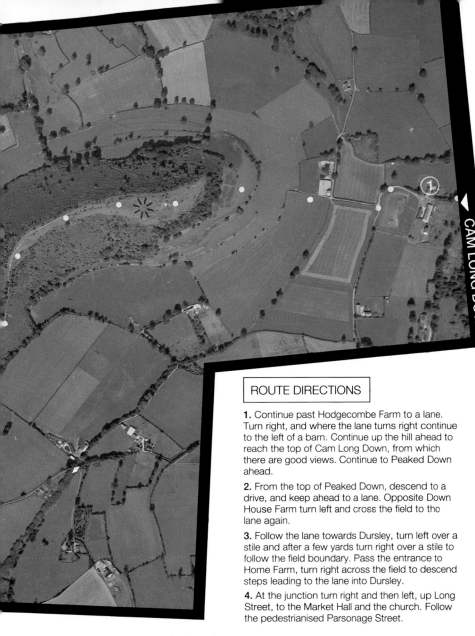

ROUTE DIRECTIONS

1. Continue past Hodgecombe Farm to a lane. Turn right, and where the lane turns right continue to the left of a barn. Continue up the hill ahead to reach the top of Cam Long Down, from which there are good views. Continue to Peaked Down ahead.

2. From the top of Peaked Down, descend to a drive, and keep ahead to a lane. Opposite Down House Farm turn left and cross the field to the lane again.

3. Follow the lane towards Dursley, turn left over a stile and after a few yards turn right over a stile to follow the field boundary. Pass the entrance to Home Farm, turn right across the field to descend steps leading to the lane into Dursley.

4. At the junction turn right and then left, up Long Street, to the Market Hall and the church. Follow the pedestrianised Parsonage Street.

Cam Long Down, a distinctive hillock on the route

Dursley to Wotton-under-Edge
8½ miles (13.5km)

In this section the walker travels from one cloth town to another, passing a private battlefield and another promontory fort. Views from the escarpment encompass the River Severn and the Forest of Dean. Refreshment can be taken at North Nibley, the half-way point.

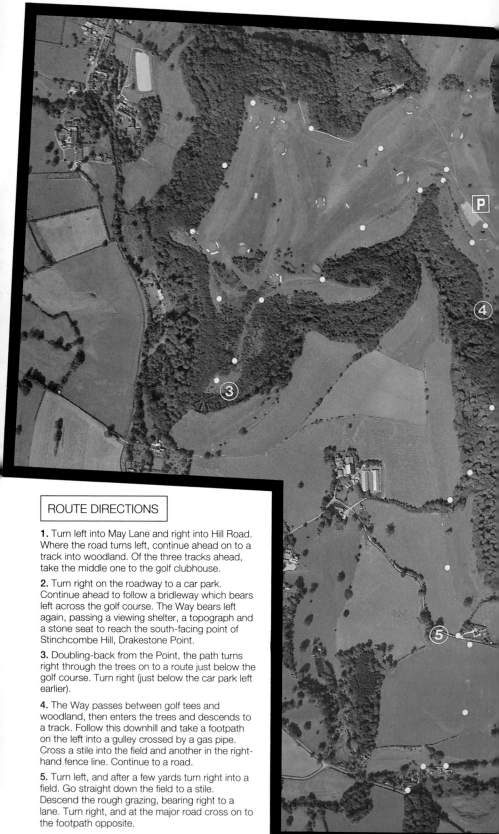

ROUTE DIRECTIONS

1. Turn left into May Lane and right into Hill Road. Where the road turns left, continue ahead on to a track into woodland. Of the three tracks ahead, take the middle one to the golf clubhouse.

2. Turn right on the roadway to a car park. Continue ahead to follow a bridleway which bears left across the golf course. The Way bears left again, passing a viewing shelter, a topograph and a stone seat to reach the south-facing point of Stinchcombe Hill, Drakestone Point.

3. Doubling-back from the Point, the path turns right through the trees on to a route just below the golf course. Turn right (just below the car park left earlier).

4. The Way passes between golf tees and woodland, then enters the trees and descends to a track. Follow this downhill and take a footpath on the left into a gulley crossed by a gas pipe. Cross a stile into the field and another in the right-hand fence line. Continue to a road.

5. Turn left, and after a few yards turn right into a field. Go straight down the field to a stile. Descend the rough grazing, bearing right to a lane. Turn right, and at the major road cross on to the footpath opposite.

THE VILLAGE OF STINCHCOMBE lies at the foot of the hill, below the seat and topograph dedicated to Sir Stanley William Tubbs who gave the land on the plateau to the public in 1930. Although only 700ft (213m) at its summit, the views from Stinchcombe Hill are excellent. If the day is clear, Exmoor, the Malvern Hills and the Brecon Beacons can be seen, as well as the monument above North Nibley on the next ascent.

Where the Way descends through a field to the main road notice a grassy rise on the right; it covers the site of a Roman villa.

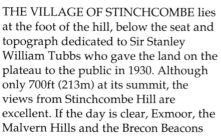

The Market Hall stands at the centre of Dursley. A statue of Queen Anne, set in a niche, faces the church

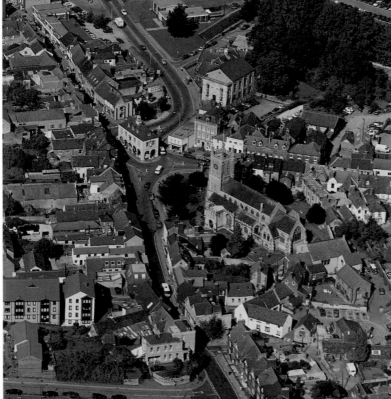

NORTH NIBLEY claims to be the birthplace of William Tyndale, and the monument to his memory, erected in 1866, towers above the village on Nibley Knoll. Tyndale had the temerity to translate the Bible into English at a time of great religious upheaval in the 1530s. He was burnt at the stake for heresy, in the Netherlands, and yet within a couple of years it was decreed that every church should be equipped with a Bible in English and others made use of his accurate translation. (Don't forget to return the key if you have admired the view from the top of the tower.)

Near the church in Nibley is Nibley Green, the scene in 1470 of the last battle to be fought in England between private armies. The cause of the dispute, in which 150 lives were lost, was due to family rivalry for the possession of the Berkeley estates.

Westridge Woods is owned by the National Trust who lets it to a forestry company. Logging operations may be encountered and there are numerous paths, but hawk-eyed observation of waymarks should keep you on course.

Brackenbury Ditches is another Iron Age hillfort but, largely obscured by woodland, it has not been excavated; it covers about 6 acres (2.4 hectares) in all.

The Tyndale Monument overlooking North Nibley

ROUTE DIRECTIONS

1. Follow the path up to some cottages. Turn left into North Nibley and at the main road junction turn right.

2. Ignoring Barrs Lane on the left, continue to a track, Wood Lane, on the left. A notice here indicates where to obtain the key to the Tyndale Monument, reached by climbing the steep-stepped path to the right. (An alternative to the steps is a more gentle ascent up the track turning right into the field and doubling back to the monument.)

3. From the monument follow the scarp edge towards Westridge Woods. Enter the wood bearing right on the track which leads past Brackenbury Ditches hillfort.

4. The Way reaches a path at the edge of the wood. Walk along the right-hand boundary of the next field and into another field.

NORTH NIBLEY

THE TREES OF THE JUBILEE CLUMP
were originally planted to celebrate the
victory of Waterloo, and later replanting
commemorated Queen Victoria's
Golden Jubilee.

Wotton-under-Edge sits on a shelf
about half way up the slope from the
Vale. Although primarily a lively
working town, it is not without
architectural merit. The gabled
almshouses beside the Falcon Hotel are

Wotton-under-Edge sprawls down the
hillside to the west of the Way

worth a visit, and compare favourably
with those encountered at Chipping
Campden. They were built with money
left to the town by Hugh Perry, a
wealthy merchant born in Wotton who
became Sheriff of London in 1632.
Guesthouses and inns can be found in
the town.

WOTTON-UNDER-EDGE

ROUTE DIRECTIONS

1. Continue towards the Jubilee Clump then follow the Way down to the main road. Head towards Wotton-under-Edge and turn right into Bradley Street. Continue into High Street, then Long Street.

2. Turn left into Church Street, cross the major road (note kerbstone waymark) and turn right.

Follow the alley, turning left to the church.

3. Turn right at the road and right again into Valley Road. Turn right at Ragnall Lane then left to the road in Coombe.

4. Turn right and where the road ascends and bears right, bear left into a driveway and right to Lisleway Hill.

5. Turn left and after ½ mile (800m) turn sharp right on to a track. Where the track bears left continue ahead through a gate. Go down through the field to a gate on the left. Through the gate the Way follows the contour to a track.

6. Turn right and continue downhill into a deep gulley ending at a stile. Cross this and turn left along the field edge to the road at Wortley.

HOUSES AND GARDENS

Cotswolds manor houses tend to be substantial and comfortable rather than 'stately'. Built of the same local stone as the other village houses, they fit into the scene with an easy nonchalance. Stanway House, near Broadway, was built in the golden local limestone by the Tracy family when Elizabeth I was on the throne. Its straightforward simplicity is set off by the flamboyantly grand gatehouse added in the 17th century, with bell-shaped gables topped by the carved scallop shells of the Tracy heraldic badge.

Dummy figures in Japanese armour and nightmare helmets glaring samurai-style from an upstairs bedroom make an unexpected sight, but only one of the surprises at Snowshill Manor. Outwardly a conventional time-softened mansion, it contains an extraordinary jumble of objects, assembled on the jackdaw principle by Charles Wade, who gave the house to the National Trust in 1951. An omnivorous collector, he packed it from floor to ceiling with everything he took a fancy to, from clocks, ship models and antique spectacles to Buddhas and Burmese rice jars.

Horton Court, near Chipping Sodbury, is another charming manor house, with a 12th-century hall on view. Much grander and more formal. with an east front in Bath stone, is Dyrham Park, another National Trust property. Built

Painswick House
Sudeley Castle

about 1700 for one of William III's ministers, it contains fine furniture and Dutch paintings.

Standing among massive yew hedges like bastions, Sudeley Castle, outside Winchcombe, is part house and part haunting romantic ruin. Catherine Parr, Henry VIII's widow, owned it and there is a beautiful Victorian monument to her in the church. The wealthy Dent family of Worcester glovers restored the house in the 19th century.

Notable gardens include the recently restored 18th-century rococo pleasure ground at Painswick House. Hidcote Manor Garden, outside Chipping Campden, with its succession of garden 'rooms' separated by hedges and walls, and its blend of formality and exuberance has exerted a powerful influence on contemporary garden design. Created on a bare Cotswold hillside by Lawrence Johnston, largely between the wars, it now belongs to the National Trust. Next door is the delightful garden of Kiftsgate Court, with England's largest rose. Sir Edwin Lutyens had a hand in the garden at Misarden Park, above the Golden valley near Stroud, with topiary and a traditional rose garden among its attractions.

Stanton Court

ROUTE DIRECTIONS

1. Cross the road, go over a stile and walk diagonally left across the field to a stile/gate. Continue to another stile/gate and follow the track over a stream. Turn right up Kennerwell Lane, converging on a road into Alderley.

2. At the crossroads, take the lane straight ahead to the next road junction. Bear left on the road and immediately turn left on to a track.

3. Follow the track through gates and over stiles, passing above New Mills Farm below right. The path enters a mixture of gulley and open field and passes through a gate into a sunken lane.

4. Turn right into Watery Lane (aptly named!) and out on to the road. Turn left up the Kilcott valley.

Alderley — ruin on Winner Hill

Wotton-under-Edge to Old Sodbury 10½ miles (17km)

During this part of the walk the Way crosses from Gloucestershire into the 'new' county of Avon, traversing Beaufort and Badminton country as it does so. Valleys and woodland provide a contrast to the High Wold further north. Horton Court is a pleasant place to stop before arriving at the Sodburys.

THIS IS ONE OF the remoter parts of the Way, crossing the boundary between Gloucestershire and Avon at Watery Lane.

The Kilcott valley may have a remote feel now, but would have been much busier in the days when the mills on the stream were operating. Wortley lay at the centre of a high concentration of mills used for the cloth industry and one mill race is still visible in the Kilcott valley.

Alderley is a quiet and pretty village with a number of large, handsome houses. One of these, the Grange, is where Sir Matthew Hale was born in 1609. Lord Chief Justice for five years, Hale was an eminent and highly-regarded lawyer.

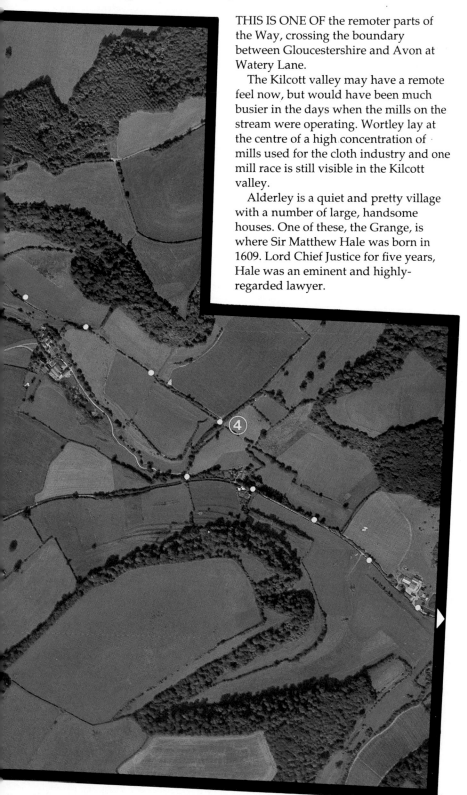

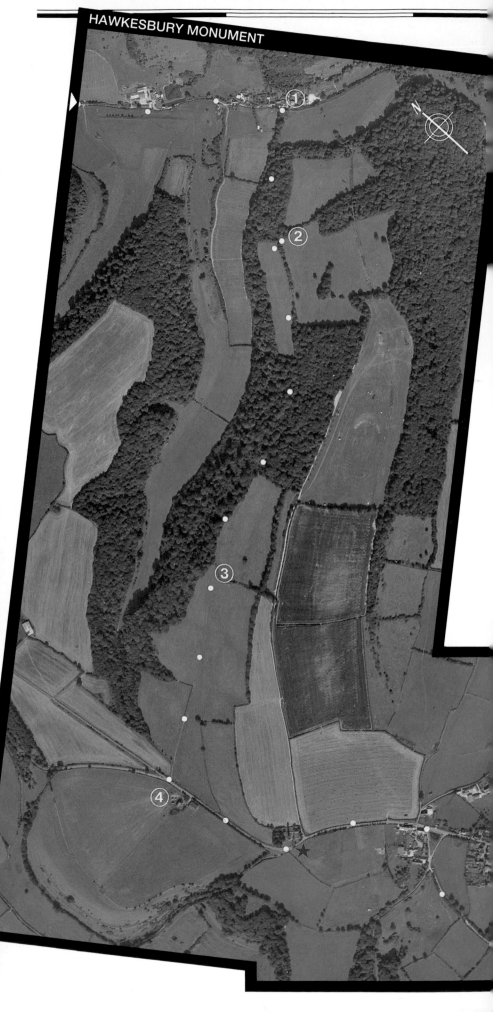

This impressive monument, just outside Hawkesbury Upton, commemorates General Somerset

THE HAWKESBURY — or Somerset — Monument was erected in 1846 in memory of General Somerset for his prowess at Waterloo. He was a member of the Beaufort family whose seat is a few miles away at Badminton, which has become famous for its annual horse trials. The monument stands just over 120ft (36.5m) high and has a viewing platform at the top.

The hamlet of Hawkesbury lies to the west, 250ft (76m) below the scarp; Hawkesbury Upton is the 'upp tunn', the upper enclosure.

ROUTE DIRECTIONS

1. At the third group of houses turn right through a gate on to a track through Greenhill Wood.

2. The Way passes through a gate and immediately right into a field. Proceed with the hedge on the left to the far end and cross a stile into Claypit Wood. Follow the waymarked route to reach a fence by a field and continue inside the woodland to a gate.

3. Out into the field, head towards the right-hand side of a barn on the horizon, eventually reaching a gate just short of the road.

4. Turn left up the road to the Hawkesbury/Somerset Monument. Continue towards Hawkesbury Upton. Ignore the left turn to Starveall, and turn right at the duck pond. This is a pleasant place to stop and picnic, or a shop and inn await the walker who diverts into the village. Just after the junction with the road from the other side of the pond, bear left into Bath Lane.

Horton Court, one of the oldest inhabited houses in the Cotswolds, and the village church

VIEWS ALONG BATH LANE open up towards the North Wessex Downs and the Vale of Severn. Another long-distance path, the Ridgeway Path, runs for 85 miles (137km) (10 miles (16km) shorter than this route) over the Downs from East Kennett near Marlborough in Wiltshire to Ivinghoe Beacon near Tring in Hertfordshire.

The National Trust acquired Horton Court, together with 146 acres (59 hectares) of adjacent farmland, in 1949. The hall, all that remains of the original fortified manor house built in the 12th century, and the detached late Perpendicular ambulatory are open to the public. In the early 16th century the main part of the house was built for William Knight, chief secretary to Henry VIII. Opening times are limited, but written appointments to visit can be made with the tenant.

A short walk through the gardens leads to Horton's church, built in the 14th century and dedicated to St James. There is a memorial inside to Anne Paston, whose family owned the Court from the 16th to the 18th centuries.

ROUTE DIRECTIONS

1. Continue along Bath Lane and into fields, keeping the boundary on the right.

2. Just before reaching Highfield Lane turn into the field on the right. The Way follows the left-hand hedge over two more stiles, then bears right down the field to a gateway. Follow the edge of the field round to the left and bear right to a stile.

3. Follow the path inside the wood to a track and turn right. Continue to a road and turn left to Horton village, where there is limited accommodation. (Turn right to visit Horton Court.)

4. At the junction, turn right and then left on to a track. Continue over a stile and into a large field.

Little Sodbury (above) and its hillfort and manor house (below)

WILLIAM TYNDALE was tutor to the children of the Walsh household at Little Sodbury Manor in the 1520s and during this time is thought to have worked on his translation of the Bible into English. As chaplain, he also preached in Little Sodbury's church, uniquely dedicated to St Adeline and at that time standing behind the manor. By 1859 the church had all but collapsed, and stone by stone it was rebuilt on the existing site closer to the village.

Sodbury hillfort, occupying 11 acres (4.5 hectares), was used long after the Iron Age by the Romans and the Saxons, and much later served as a resting place for Yorkist forces moving north for the Battle of Tewkesbury during the Wars of the Roses.

The Brooke memorial seat in Old Sodbury's churchyard is a good place to rest and view the Vale in comfort. Gilbert Edward Brooke was chief medical officer of health for Singapore from 1902 to 1928. Those seeking refreshment will be pleased to find the Dog Inn in the village.

ROUTE DIRECTIONS

1. Cross the field to a gate. Walk down below the dam of a farm reservoir and follow the next field boundary on the right to reach a stile. Cross this and turn left into the yard and garden of a private house to reach the road in Little Sodbury.

2. Turn right and then left beside the church. Along the lane, turn left to Little Sodbury Manor.

3. Bear right off the drive to a gate, then climb left on the upper track to the farm buildings above. Turn right beside them then left over a stile. Turn right through a gap in the ramparts of Sodbury hillfort.

4. Cross the hillfort to another gap opposite, then a stile. Turn right downhill and then left to follow the Way along a field boundary on the right. Pass above the farm buildings to a track which leads to the primary school and the road outside Old Sodbury church.

5. Continue through the churchyard and walk down the field to a stile in the left corner. Bear half-right towards a stile/gate. Enter a farmyard and follow the path to the A432.

FARMING

The Cotswolds farming landscape of today, with its wheatfields and pastures separated by drystone walls, is essentially the creation of the last three centuries. Before that there were huge open sheep-walks and arable fields hundreds of acres in extent, growing barley, wheat and oats, and manured by the sheep, which part of the time were folded on the arable. The sheep flocks were vast. It has been estimated that in the early 1200s there were half a million animals grazing in the pastures. In the 14th century the acreage of arable declined and the number of sheep grew; partly because of the depopulation caused by the Black Death, which is said to have carried off half the population of Gloucestershire. More than 50 lost villages have been identified on the Cotswolds, a few silent humps and hollows in the ground showing where once families lived, worked and died.

The wealth of the Cotswolds grew on the backs of its sheep. Some belonged to the local farmers, some were part of the herds owned by monasteries and ecclesiastical landlords – Tewkesbury Abbey, Winchcombe Abbey, the Bishop of Worcester and others.

Sheep are still to be seen on the

Typical farmland outside Winchcombe

The Cotswold breed

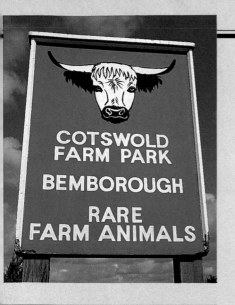

Cotswold slopes, though they tend to be outnumbered by cattle nowadays. The burly traditional 'Cotswold Lions' can be seen today in the Cotswold Farm Park, near Guiting Power. They have white faces and black nostrils, broad backs and heavy bodies – heavy enough to need strong shearers to handle them. Since the 18th century they have been crossed with Leicesters, Dorsets and other breeds to improve the stock.

Down on the clay in the Vale of Severn, sheltered between the Cotswolds and the Welsh hills, lush fields support dairy and beef herds, orchards and market gardens. Before the coming of the railways in the 19th century, beef cattle from the Vale were

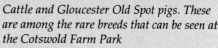

Cattle and Gloucester Old Spot pigs. These are among the rare breeds that can be seen at the Cotswold Farm Park

driven up to London in bellowing herds. It was their milk that went to make the Single and Double Gloucester cheeses of yore. There are few left today.

Another prized Vale product was the Gloucester Old Spot pig, lop-eared and white with black spots and thick hair. It was the traditional orchard and cottager's pig. A few are still bred, although they have fewer spots than their redoubtable ancestors.

In this century, farming in the area has followed the same trends as elsewhere: mechanisation, much bigger farms and heavy use of artificial fertilisers. Standardisation and factory methods have made the old ways increasingly obsolete.

Old Sodbury to Cold Ashton

9 miles (14.5km)

From the Sodburys the Way passes through the Dodington Estate, originally founded on profits from sugar. The old Saxon kingdom of Mercia then gives way to Wessex before the walker passes the parkland of a stately home built for a secretary to William III. There is more road walking in this stretch than previously encountered, but this is compensated for by the relatively level, easy going and pleasant villages where it is possible to stop and have a drink.

DODINGTON

Old Sodbury

ROUTE DIRECTIONS

1. Cross the A432 into Chapel Lane and shortly pass over the railway tunnel carrying the main line from London to Wales. Continue, to enter fields on the left. Strike diagonally right up the slope to Catchpot cottage in Coombes End.

2. Turn right and just beyond the junction turn left into a field. Aim for two stiles either side of a drive and strike uphill towards woodland. The landowner has marked the Way with white-topped posts.

3. Cross the stile by the gate between two woods and follow the path beside the wood on the left. Where the wood ends continue ahead to a footbridge, and then bear left towards a gate.

DODINGTON PARK was the seat of the Codrington family for 250 years. Christopher Codrington made a fortune during the 17th century from sugar plantations in the West Indies and the house was rebuilt by him at the end of the 18th century to a design by James Wyatt, who also worked on Broadway Tower. Capability Brown had landscaped the park some 50 years earlier. Very secluded and not visible from the Way, the house, one of the largest in the Cotswolds, has not been open to the public since the estate was sold a decade ago. Pheasant and guinea fowl from the estate can often be seen crossing the path.

Built by James Wyatt in 1795, Dodington House lies near the Way but is not visible from the path

The county boundary between Avon and Wiltshire lies just to the east of Tormarton

ROUTE DIRECTIONS

1. Continue to the A46. Cross the road with care to a stone stile. Walk across fields and two village roads before reaching a third road at a bend.

2. Turn left and after a few yards turn right over a slab stile and head for the stile opposite the church in Tormarton.

3. Turn right on the road, and right again at the road junction. Just beyond the Portcullis Inn, turn left into a drive and then go ahead to a stile. Cross the field to a stile and turn left to another. Do not cross this stile, but turn right keeping the wall on your left to reach a road.

4. Turn right to join another road which reaches the A46. Turn left, and then negotiate the maelstrom of the M4 junction. Keep to the left, crossing the entry and exit slip roads with the bridge in between. Continue on the left-hand verge to a layby.

5. The waymark directs you across the road. Turn left along the verge to reach another layby, and turn right to the picnic area.

6. Leave by the vehicle access road, crossing the old A46 to a footpath opposite leading into a strip of woodland.

7. Turn left to follow the field edge as it bends right to a gate. Turn left and keep to the hedge on the right.

STONE STILES are a common feature in the Cotswolds, and around Tormarton there are plenty. Some in fact are modern concrete substitutes and the original quarried stone variety, which are becoming increasingly rare, are now being listed. For reasons of cost, most new houses are also being built of coloured concrete, or from blocks made from a mixture of sand and crushed stone. Roofing slates, too, are moulded in concrete to resemble stone, but the traditional style of Cotswold architecture is largely being followed.

These days only a few quarries are worked, and abandoned quarries can be seen all over the area, usually just outside a village.

It is worth going inside the church of St Mary Magdalene at Tormarton to look at the memorials, in particular the brass of John Ceysill who, it is recorded, died in 1493. The Jacobean pulpit is also of interest, and there are some intriguing gargoyles.

The Tormarton picnic area, with its toilet block, is utilitarian rather than scenic, but nevertheless comes as a welcome rest point to the walker.

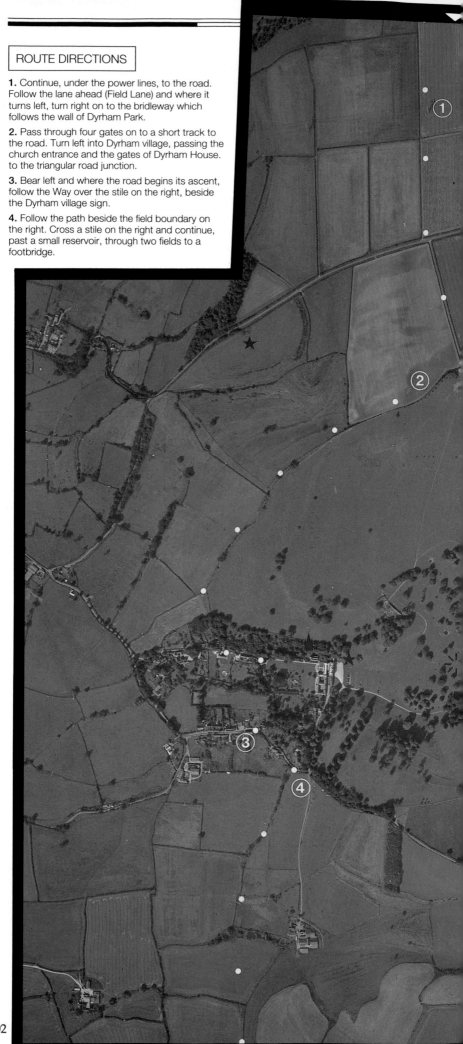

ROUTE DIRECTIONS

1. Continue, under the power lines, to the road. Follow the lane ahead (Field Lane) and where it turns left, turn right on to the bridleway which follows the wall of Dyrham Park.

2. Pass through four gates on to a short track to the road. Turn left into Dyrham village, passing the church entrance and the gates of Dyrham House. to the triangular road junction.

3. Bear left and where the road begins its ascent, follow the Way over the stile on the right, beside the Dyrham village sign.

4. Follow the path beside the field boundary on the right. Cross a stile on the right and continue, past a small reservoir, through two fields to a footbridge.

TO THE NORTH of the wall of Dyrham Park notice the strip lynchets — ridges formed on hillsides from ancient ploughing. Above are the slopes of Hinton Hill, crowned with an old hillfort. In 577AD this was the site of the Battle of Dyrham, during which the West Saxons Cuthwine and Cealwin defeated and slew three Celtic princes, Coinmail, Condidan and Farinmail. As a result, the Vale of the Severn was opened up to Saxon influence as far as Gloucester, and the Britons were pushed further west towards Cornwall and Wales.

Originally a much more modest Tudor mansion, Dyrham House was extensively rebuilt by William Blathwayt, whose descendants own the estate at Porlock in Devon.

Blathwayt was Secretary of War and Secretary of State to William III and Queen Anne from 1691 to 1710 and the diarist, John Evelyn, described him thus: 'This gentleman is Secretary of War, Clerk of the Council, etc, having raised himself by his industry from very moderate circumstances. He is a very proper, handsome person, very dextrous in business, and, besides all this, has married a great fortune'. The house has hardly been changed at all since Blathwayt's day, and retains the original fabric and furnishings.

The park, consisting of 263 acres (106.4 hectares), is home to a herd of fallow deer thought to be among the oldest in the country. From the top of the hill there are panoramic views stretching across to Bristol. House and park now belong to the National Trust; the park is open all year, but the house during the summer only. Access is only available from the main entrance on the A46.

Dyrham House and the parish church

Vernacular architecture in Cold Ashton. The church has many interesting features, including a squint

TOGHILL LANE lies on the Jurassic Way, which links the south-west with Lincolnshire. Almost opposite Cold Ashton Manor, a footpath waymarked along St Catharine's valley to the left forms part of the Limestone Link which bypasses Bath to meet the West Mendip Way above Wells.

Cold Ashton Manor is hidden from view behind its wall and Renaissance gateway and a better view can be obtained by walking down the Limestone Link into the field below. (From here the village rectory can also be seen, to the right of the manor.) The original house was owned by Bath Abbey until the Dissolution of the Monasteries and it is thought that the present building was begun towards the end of the 16th century. Despite later restoration, it remains a fine example of Elizabethan architecture.

ROUTE DIRECTIONS

1. From the footbridge continue ahead, entering Dyrham Wood at the corner of the field.

2. The path through the wood emerges into a field. Proceed up the field, passing to the right of a walled enclosure, to Toghill Lane, which is unexpectedly busy.

3. Go left along the road for a short distance then turn right into a field, keeping the hedge on the right to reach an enclosed green lane. Continue past cottages to reach the A46 at Pennsylvania, where refreshments can be obtained.

4. Cross the busy road and go over a stile into a field at the end of the buildings. Aim diagonally right up the field to the far corner.

5. Go over the stone stile and bear diagonally left across the field to a gate on to the A420 Bristol to Chippenham road. Keep on the left to the White Hart Inn.

6. Cross the road and continue to the church. From the church follow the path to the road in Cold Ashton. Turn right past the Manor through the village. Where a major road turns right, bear left down to the A46. Cross over into Greenway Lane straight ahead.

ABBEYS AND CHURCHES

Pilgrims in the Middle Ages made their way reverently to Hailes Abbey, near Winchcombe, to venerate a famous relic – a phial of the Holy Blood. It was denounced as a fake in 1539, when the Cistercian monastery was closed down and treated as a supply yard for building stone. Today the surviving cloisters stand in an idyllic setting below the Cotswolds edge. Of another Cistercian abbey at Kingswood, near Wotton-under-Edge, only the gatehouse is left. The abbey church at Bath was not completed until long after the Dissolution.

In the southern Cotswolds outstanding Norman churches include Elkston and Leonard Stanely, with a

The church of St James the Great in Chipping Campden

Norman tower and a riot of carving inside. There is more Norman work at Avening, where the visitor can also admire the piously kneeling effigy of Henry Brydges, a notorious highwayman and smuggler who died in 1615. For monuments, however, there is nothing to surpass the colossal memorials of the Dukes of Beaufort at Great Badminton.

The great 'wool churches' are the glory of the Cotswolds. They were built in the 15th century, when four influences joined hands: wool trade profits, the mellow local stone, a long tradition of skilled masonry, and the sumptuous Perpendicular style of architecture, which first flowered at Gloucester Cathedral.

Perhaps the most spectacular example is the spacious, light-filled church of St James the Great at Chipping Campden, with its slender columns and its tremendous, embattled tower. There is another heroic tower at St Peter's, Winchcombe, which is adorned with grotesque heads and gargoyles. (Henry Ford wanted to buy the church and take it to America.)

Smaller churches, too, nestling amoung their attendant villages, have their own fascinations. At Sevenhampton in the Coln valley the central tower is startlingly supported by flying buttresses inside the church. At Buckland, near Broadway, the church has work of every century from the 13th to the 17th, and a 15th-century rectory. At Stanway the church forms part of a famously photogenic group with the manor house and cottages. St Kenelm's at Alderley, near Wotton-under-Edge, was rebuilt at the beginning of the 19th century in the 'Gothic' taste.

From this century, All Saints at Uplands, a suburb of Stroud, is a beautiful Edwardian church by Temple Moore. The medieval village church at Stanton was glowingly refurnished between the wars by Sir Ninian Comper. Prinknash Abbey was built after the Second World War for a Benedictine community.

About 40 gargoyles can be seen on Winchcombe's church

Prinknash Abbey, functional rather than decorative

The scant remains of Hailes Abbey

Cold Ashton to Bath 10 miles (16km)

On this last leg of the journey the route sweeps round in a semi-circle, gradually dropping down into the suburbs of Bath. Before reaching the city, the Way passes its last hillfort, its last topograph and its last two golf courses. More fine views and a varied landscape await the walker.

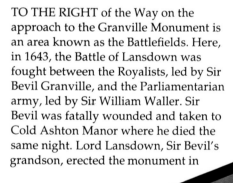

TO THE RIGHT of the Way on the approach to the Granville Monument is an area known as the Battlefields. Here, in 1643, the Battle of Lansdown was fought between the Royalists, led by Sir Bevil Granville, and the Parliamentarian army, led by Sir William Waller. Sir Bevil was fatally wounded and taken to Cold Ashton Manor where he died the same night. Lord Lansdown, Sir Bevil's grandson, erected the monument in 1720. It is interesting to note from the inscriptions, mentioning Granville, Grenville and Grenvile, how the spelling of names can change.

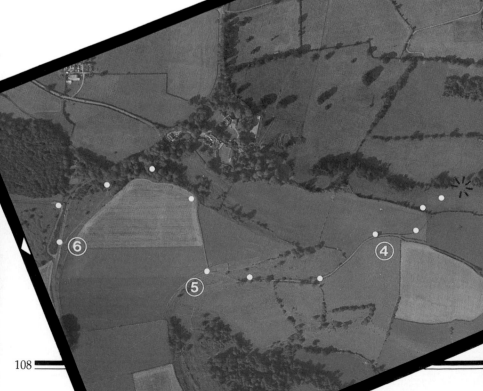

ROUTE DIRECTIONS

1. Continue past Hill Farm. In the valley bottom take the path ahead, through trees, to an open field.

Battlefields, near Lower Hamswell

2. Cross three fields to reach a road beside a cottage and turn left. Go over the cattle grids, then look for a waymark on the right.

3. The seat in the next field was donated by the owner of Lilliput Farm, which can be seen across the valley. Cross the stile above and follow the hedge round to the right to reach a green lane (Langridge Lane).

4. Turn right and where the lane emerges into a field bear right uphill to a stile in a wall.

5. Follow the wall on the right, then descend into woodland, veering left by a wall to reach a stile before turning left to the Granville Monument.

6. Cross the road south of the monument on to a path to follow the access road to the monitoring station.

ROUTE DIRECTIONS

1. Continue to the right of the monitoring station and turn left. Proceed to a junction of paths at Hanging Hill, by the trig point (771ft, 235m).

2. Turn sharp left over the stile and follow the scarp edge on to the golf course. Head through the pines to reach a track. Bear left beside the woodland, crossing a drive to reach a path junction. Turn right.

3. Follow the bridleway downhill, bearing left at a waymark post. Beyond the gate, walk below the embankment of Little Down hillfort.

4. Turn sharp left to enter the hillfort. Beyond the rear embankment turn right. Turn left at the corner of the field, cross a stile and proceed past Bath racecourse to Prospect Stile and a topograph.

5. Cross the stile and turn left to reach a track. Turn right to the junction, turn left through gates, then turn right into a field. Keep the hedge on your right.

LITTLE DOWN HILLFORT is the last of the promontory forts passed by walkers of the Way and here a well-defined ditch and rampart are still evident. It marks the most westerley point on the Way.

On leaving Bath racecourse we also reach the last topograph of the walk. This one was erected by the Cotswold Voluntary Warden Service based at Bath, and paid for from donations by well-wishers who have enjoyed the guided walks and lectures organised by the service. Views from here encompass Kelston Round Hill to the south, with its characteristic clump of trees. The hill is reminiscent of May Hill, seen across the Severn beyond Gloucester.

Most of the Cotswold Way lies on the watershed between the Thames and the River Severn but now the River Avon, which rises to the east of the scarp near Old Sodbury, comes into view. The Avon circles round Malmesbury, Chippenham, Melksham and Bradford-on- Avon before following the Limpley Stoke valley into Bath and on to Bristol.

N

Little Down

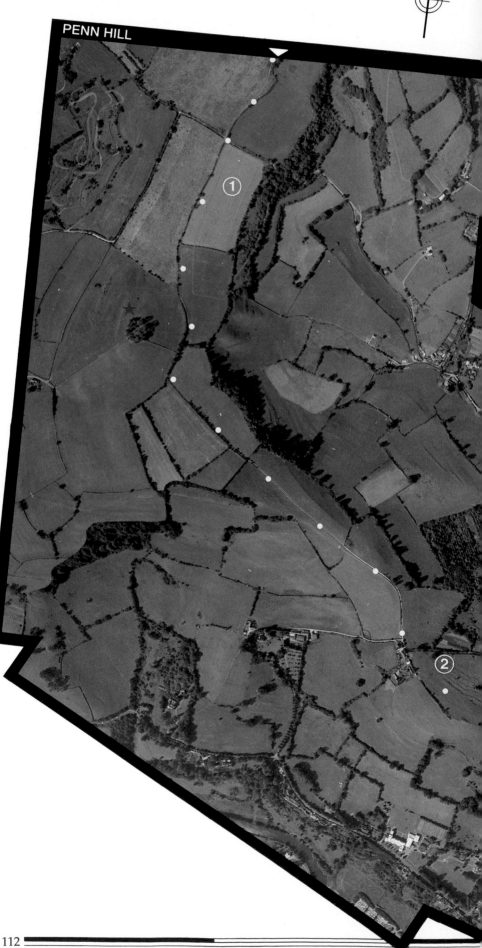

1. Continue along the track through a gate, using the boardwalk and separated pedestrian sections on the right if the bridleway is muddy. At the crossroads at Pendean Farm, continue ahead over the stile immediately to the left of the farm.

2. Follow the wall on the right to a stile, along an enclosed path and downhill to the last trig point (397ft, 121m) of the Way on Penn Hill. After crossing two stiles walk straight across the recreation ground to the far corner.

3. Turn left on the road, pass an estate road and go down a small left-hand lane to cross the main road in Weston near the shops. Turn right along the terrace of Church Street, bearing left up to the churchyard. (From Weston it is possible to take a bus into Bath.)

4. Pass to the right of the church on to the road. Turn left and then turn right into Purlewent Drive. Follow the footway (ignore road to the right) and bear left into a close and then an alleyway between and round the back of the houses.

ALONG THIS STRETCH of the walk views towards Bath open up, starting with the suburb of Weston to the left which gradually creeps up the valley below Lansdown. Above Weston, the Beckford Monument can be seen on the horizon and below, to the right, is Lansdown Crescent. From Penn Hill the expanse of industrial Bath with its gas holders and factories is evident in the Avon valley bottom — a side of the city of which most visitors are unaware.

The square tower of Bath Abbey, our destination, contrasts with the spire of the Roman Catholic church of St John nearby, and the city's position at the confluence of several valleys is clear. The possibility of industrial spread — as at Stroud — prompted local authorities to press for the official Cotswolds Area of Outstanding Natural Beauty to be extended to include the hillsides above Bath.

Although Weston is now a suburb of Bath, the heart of the old village still exists around the church, inside which is a memorial to Dr William Oliver, who 'invented' the Bath Oliver biscuit. Purlewent Drive, nearby, is named after Samuel Purlewent, an attorney in London and freeman of the city of Bath.

BATH

ROUTE DIRECTIONS

1. On emerging from Purlewent Drive the Way passes through its last field before entering the main conurbation of Bath. Go up the alleyway to a road and cross to another alleyway to reach Summerhill Road.

2. Turn right into Sion Hill. This bends to the left, and where it bends to the left again beyond Ormonde House, turn right down the footpath over High Common.

3. Cross Weston Road into Royal Victoria Park. Continue ahead to a junction and turn left to the Victoria Memorial. Cross the road below Marlborough Buildings, then go through a gateway into the Royal Avenue with the Royal Crescent above on the left.

4. Continue down the hill into Queen's Square. Turn left to pass the Francis Hotel and go ahead into Wood Street then Quiet Street.

5. Turn right into Milsom Street and left into New Bond Street. Take New Bond Street Place on the right to Upper Borough Walls and walk to Cheap Street.

6. Go through the archway opposite and into the churchyard of Bath Abbey — journey's end.

BATH

Visitors have been coming to Bath for more than 2,000 years, since before the Roman times. Today's ravishing Georgian town was planned to restore the grandeur of Roman days. The dignified classical terraces and parades, squares and crescents, which line the steep side of the Avon valley were built of honeyed Bath stone, a variety of oolitic limestone quarried in the nearby hills. Thought beautiful to look at, it is all too prone to damage by rain and smoke.

The main architects of Georgian Bath were the two John Woods, father and son. The stately Royal Crescent is generally considered the younger Wood's masterpiece and Number One has been furnished to show what the houses were like inside when Bath was a smart resort in the days of patches and periwigs, footmen and sedan chairs.

Pulteney Bridge, lined with shops, is one of the city's showpieces

Society came to Bath to bathe in or drink the water of the hot spring, which bubbles up at the rate of about one million litres a day at a steady temperature of 46.5°C. At the elegant 1790s Pump Room, which says 'water is best' in Greek on the outside, you can try a glass of the spring water (it tastes repulsive). Immediately underneath are the remains of the Roman Spa, which was developed here from the 1st century on. The focus of the complex is the majestic King's bath.

Much of the pleasure of Bath is gained by simply walking about and admiring it, but there is no shortage of individual attractions. The abbey church is known for its fan-vaulting and its many memorial tablets to 18th-century fashionables, including Beau Nash, the famous master of ceremonies. You can enjoy a traditional Bath bun at Sally Lunn's nearby. Pulteney Bridge over the Avon was designed by Robert Adam.

The Holbourne of Menstrie Museum's elegant 18th-century building contains beautifully displayed collections of paintings, porcelain, silver and glass. The Museum of Costume in the Assembly Rooms has one of the world's largest collections of its kind. The Royal Photographic Society in the Octagon in Milsom Street has engaging displays on the history of photography. At Camden Works in Julian Road you can gaze in alarm at J.B. Bowler's maniacally dangerous 19th-century engineering works, and don't miss the delicious collections of English naive art in the Paragon. The annual Bath Festival of music and the arts has an international reputation.

Even beautiful Bath has not escaped industrial and housing development

The Circus was built over a period of 20 years by the Woods, father and son

Index

Index to places along the Cotswold Way

Useful Organisations

The following bodies may be contacted at the addresses given for any further information required.

Countryside Commission, John Dower House, Crescent Place, Cheltenham, Gloucestershire GL50 3RA

Forestry Commission, 231 Corstorphine Road, Edinburgh EH12 7AT

National Trust, 36 Queen Anne's Gate, London SW1H 9AS

English Nature, Northminster House, Peterborough, Cambridgeshire PE1 1UA

English Heritage, Spur 17, Government Buildings, Hawkenbury, Tunbridge Wells, Kent TN2 5AQ

Long Distance Walkers' Association, Lodgefield Cottage, High Street, Flimwell, Wadhurst, East Sussex TN5 7PH

Ramblers' Association, 1/5 Wandsworth Road, London SW8 2XX

Youth Hostels Association, Trevelyan House, 8 St Stephens Hill, St Albans, Herts AL1 2DY

The Cotswold Countryside Service, Gloucestershire County Council, County Planning Department, Shire Hall, Gloucester GL1 8BR

Heart of England Tourist Board, Woodside, Larkhill, Worcester WR5 2EF

The Gloucestershire Trust for Nature Conservation, Robinswood Hill Country Park, Reservoir Road, Gloucester

Downham Hill

Charlton Kings Common